An Introduction To Theosophy

Sriram Rajagopal

Cover image and illustrations by
Jeanne d'Arc Jabbour

Published by
Sriram Rajagopal

Layout and typeset in Lucida 32/ 24 and Sans pro 11/10
ISBN: 979-88-6757-709-4

Dedication

To my Teacher, Grand Master Choa Kok Sui
and to my *sangha*, my spiritual family.

Acknowledgements

To my Teacher, Grand Master Choa Kok Sui.
Without his teachings and his guidance,
I would not be who I am today.

To all the Teachers and authors of the Theosophical Society,
Mme Blavatsky, Annie Besant, C W Leadbeater,
Geoffrey Hodson and I K Taimni, to name a few.

To my mother, who initiated my interest in spirituality,
and who continues to inspire me with her
strength and discipline.

To my wife, my best friend, my guide,
my creative inspiration, my *kilshi*.

Table of Contents

Foreword

Why another book on Theosophy? There are already so many books, written by extremely learned and highly evolved teachers. Do we really need one more?

My decision to write this book came down to three factors.

First, the language used around one hundred years ago was very different from what we use today. I have found that many people find the language and vocabulary used a bit difficult to understand. Hence, my first objective was to write this book in simple English, following the style of my own teacher, Grand Master Choa Kok Sui.

Secondly, I wanted to add many more illustrations. While there are some illustrations in the original books, with modern computer technology, I felt that we can add many more illustrations to help understand the teachings. As the saying goes, a picture is worth a thousand words.

Finally, I wanted to write the book in the way I find it easiest to understand the teachings. Trying to ensure that every new term and concept is introduced and explained before going into further details, and not assuming any prior knowledge.

One of my pet peeves when reading some books is the statement by the author, "As is well known . . ." I have always wondered who it is that knows, because I certainly do not know and most people that I know, do not know either!

In this book, I have tried to avoid any such expectation, explaining topics and terminologies in as simple a way as possible, following a flow which will hopefully make it easier to understand the concepts.

Having said all this, Theosophy does take time to understand. I have been studying books on Theosophy for more than thirty years now and still gain clarity each time I read the books.

My request to you is to persevere. Read the book and re-read it, read other introductory books; personally, I find *A Textbook of Theosophy* by C W Leadbeater and *A Study in Consciousness* by Annie Besant to be excellent books. Each time we read one of the books, we get more clarity and a deeper understanding.

I would be remiss if I did not thank all the people who have helped with bringing this book to its final form, my wife, Jeanne d'Arc Jabbour for creating all the illustrations, designing the cover and proofreading; Maria Liasides and Muneera Obaidli for sharing detailed inputs and suggestions to improve the clarity and flow of the text, not once, but over several drafts.

I hope you enjoy reading this book as much as I have enjoyed writing it.

Sriram Rajagopal

Chapter 1
Spirit and Matter

Spirit – Three Aspects of God

In many religions, God is represented as a Trinity, for example in Christianity, God the Father, God the Son and God the Holy Spirit. In Hinduism Shiva, Vishnu and Brahma. These three aspects represent the three primary qualities or energies of God – will (or power), love and active intelligence (which is also linked to creation; as my teacher, Grand Master Choa Kok Sui said, "You need intelligence to create!").

In Islam, the Ninety-Nine Names of Allah symbolise ninety-nine qualities of God. Allah Al Muqtadir (the all-powerful) is the will aspect, Allah Al Wadud (the all-loving) is the love aspect and Allah Al Aleem (the all-knowing) is the intelligence aspect (Allah Al Khaaliq – the Creator – is the creative aspect).

This does not mean there are three Gods, there is only one Supreme God who manifests many qualities.

We can understand this using light as an example. Imagine the Supreme God symbolised by white light. We learn in science that there are three primary colours, when it comes to light, these are red, green, and blue. These three colours can be thought of as representing the three aspects of God.

The three primary colours are derived from white light, and when combined, they form white light again. Three manifesting from one and going back to one (Fig. 1).

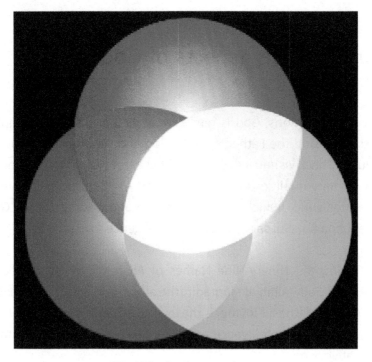

Fig. 1 The 3 primary colours

In the same way, the three aspects of God are three qualities of the Supreme God, they come from God, they return to God, they are God. There is only one Supreme God.

In the Upanishads, *Brahman* is said to be beyond our ability to comprehend and beyond description. Yet, some of the qualities of *Brahman* that are described are *sat*, *chit* and *ananda*. These are the same three qualities – *sat* (existence) is linked to will, *chit* (consciousness) is linked to intelligence and *ananda* (bliss) is linked to love.

In Theosophy, the three aspects of God are called the Three Logoi[1] - the First Logos represents will, the Second Logos, love and the Third Logos, active intelligence (Fig. 2).

The aspects of will and power are often considered together, they are like two sides of the same coin (symbolised in Hinduism by Shiva-Shakti). Similarly, the aspects of creation and intelligence are combined. This is symbolised in Hinduism by Brahma-Saraswati. (Vishnu-Lakshmi complete the Trinity. Vishnu symbolises the quality of love, the Preserver, and Lakshmi is the Goddess of prosperity and abundance.)

The three aspects of God have different roles in the process of creation, which we will study in this book.

---

[1] The word Logoi is the plural of Logos, which means 'word' in Greek. This is connected to the phrase in the Bible, "In the beginning was the Word, and the Word was with God, and the Word was God." John 1:1

This is also linked to the sound of creation, *Om*, and to the phrase in the Krishna Yajur Veda, "In the beginning was *Brahman* with whom was the Word, and the Word was truly the Supreme *Brahman*."

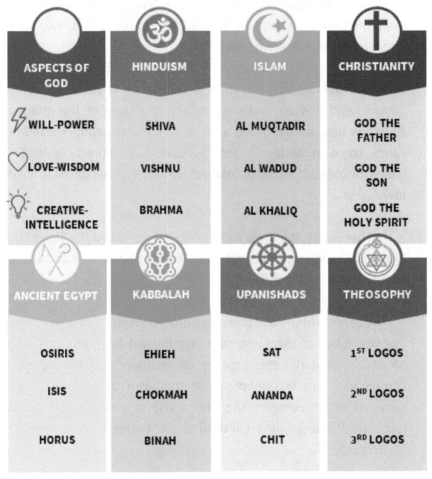

Fig. 2 Aspects of God in different traditions and religions

The process begins with the Third Logos (Brahma, Allah Al Khaaliq, God the Holy Spirit) with what is called the first outpouring– this first step creates the worlds that we live in.

The next step involves the Second Logos (Vishnu, Allah Al Wadud, God the Son) and the second outpouring. This brings in the inhabitants of the worlds that have been created.

The third step involves the First Logos (Shiva, Allah Al Muqtadir, God the Father) and the third outpouring. This is different from the other two outpourings, because it is separate for each human being. All this will be explained in the coming chapters.

Matter

When we think of the world around us, we think of the visible world – made up of solids, liquids, and gases. However, there are many more invisible worlds around us, made of subtle matter that we cannot see, except with clairvoyant sight.

This subtle matter is of several levels, the first of which is called etheric matter. Some people have heard of the human aura, this is sometimes called the etheric body because it is made of etheric matter.

More subtle than etheric matter is astral matter (also called emotional matter). And beyond that is mental matter. We are told that there are seven types of matter around us, each one more subtle than the other.

Each type of matter is made up of atoms, for example, all etheric matter is made of etheric atoms, all astral matter is made of astral atoms[2], and so forth. Let us look at how all this matter came to exist.

---

[2] The word 'atom' comes from the Greek word *atomos* which means indivisible, it is the smallest particle that can exist. An etheric atom is the smallest particle of etheric matter, an astral atom is the smallest particle of astral matter, etc.

In The Beginning Was . . .

Let us study the formation of our solar system. The aspect of God that created and sustains our solar system is called the Solar Logos or Solar God or Solar *Parabrahman*.

As Grand Master Choa Kok Sui says:
"There is only one Supreme God who is Omnipresent. The presence of the Supreme God in the sun and in the solar system is called the Solar God, Solar Parabrahman."
The Existence of God is Self-Evident

When our Solar Logos decided to create the solar system, He did not start with nothing. There was already matter that existed. Not matter as we know it today, not even the subtle matter that makes up our subtle bodies or auras, this is matter so subtle, that it is difficult for even most clairvoyants to perceive (this is what is known as *prakriti* in the *Samkhya* tradition).

> The *Samkhya* tradition says there is an eternal duality, *purusha* (meaning 'person' representing consciousness) exists separately from *prakriti* or matter. However, several Upanishads say there is only one reality, *Brahman*. As Grand Master Choa Kok Sui says, there are different levels of truth. Perhaps the *Samkhya* system is describing reality from the perspective of our solar system, where consciousness and matter exist separately, while the Upanishads are describing reality at the ultimate level, beyond the galaxy, the universe and universes, where there is only one reality, *Brahman*.

In some Theosophy books, this root matter is called bubbles in *koilon*. It is the ultimate building block of our solar system.

The first step our Solar Logos takes is to establish a boundary in space, demarcating what will be the future solar system. Think of this as a fence, everything inside the fence is part of His property (or His manifestation), anything outside the fence is not. This 'fence' is called the Solar Ring-Pass-Not in some books.

First Outpouring (First Life Wave)

The Third Logos (the active intelligence aspect of the Solar Logos) sends His energy (or His life to use another term) into all the matter within the 'fence' or Ring-Pass-Not. This is called the first outpouring or first life wave.

This causes the matter within the Ring-Pass-Not to become different from the matter outside, because the matter within is now infused with the life / energy of the Third Logos.

> To understand this concept, let us consider our own body. It is alive because all the cells (or atoms) that make up our body are filled with the energy or life of the soul that occupies the body. (We will discuss the nature of the soul in a later chapter.) When the soul leaves the body, we say that the body is dead. The energy of the soul in the body is literally the life of the body.

> In a similar manner, the matter within the ring-pass-not is infused with the energy or life of the Third Logos – thus, the matter within the solar system is literally His body, infused with His energy or life. Everything that exists in the solar system, the planets, the moons, animals, plants, human beings are all made of matter that constitutes the body of our Solar Logos. Hence the statement in the Bible, "For in Him, we live, and move, and have our being." Acts 17:28

The energy of the Third Logos (the first life wave) causes the root matter to combine into bigger forms.

Imagine the cube in the Fig. 3 represents root matter – it is the building block of everything in our solar system and there are innumerable such building blocks available for our Solar Logos to use.

Fig. 3 Atom of the divine plane

The first step is the combination of these cubes into groups of forty-nine. Not all cubes are combined, many are left as individual cubes, but the rest are combined into groups of forty-nine (Fig. 4).

The single cubes are the atoms of what we call the divine plane or *adi* plane. This divine plane is composed of the most subtle matter in our solar system, it is completely beyond our senses and even beyond the subtle senses of most clairvoyants.

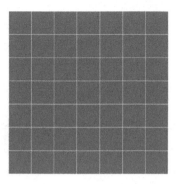

Fig. 4 Atom of the monadic plane
(49 divine plane atoms combined)

The combinations of forty-nine cubes form the building blocks or atoms of the next plane, the second plane of our solar system called the monadic plane or *anupadaka* plane. Therefore, one monadic atom is actually a combination of forty-nine divine atoms (one divine atom is represented by a single cube, one monadic atom is represented by forty-nine of these cubes combined.)[3]

The process continues and forty-nine monadic plane atoms combine to form the building block or the atom of the third plane, called the spiritual plane or *atmic* plane. Once again, not all monadic atoms are combined, many are left untouched, and the rest are combined.

---

[3] Consider a mobile phone. From our perspective, it is a single unit, a mobile phone. For a technician, it is many units put together, the screen, the case, the battery, etc. Similarly, from the perspective of the monadic plane, the forty-nine cubes combined together form a single unit, an atom of the monadic plane. Yet from the perspective of the divine plane, we see that it is actually made of forty-nine divine plane atoms.

One *atmic* atom is made of forty-nine monadic atoms combined, however, each of the monadic atoms is itself made of forty-nine divine atoms combined. Therefore:

1 *atmic* atom = 49 monadic atoms = 49X49 (2,401) divine atoms.

- Atom of the divine plane (root matter of our solar system).

- Atom of the monadic plane composed of 49 atoms of the divine plane.

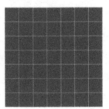

- Atom of the *atmic* plane composed of 49 monadic atoms or 49X49 divine plane atoms.

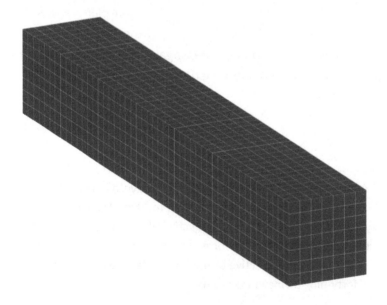

There is only one ultimate atom, one ultimate building block, but the combinations of this building block in groups of forty-nine create the atoms or building blocks of the other planes in which we exist.

Taking this further we have:

49 spiritual / *atmic* atoms	1 *buddhic* / intuitional plane atom
49 *buddhic* / intuitional plane atoms	1 mental plane atom
49 mental plane atoms	1 astral plane atom
49 astral plane atoms	1 etheric atom (ultimate atom of the physical plane)

The etheric atom is not the atom we study in physics, it is many times more subtle; it is made of 49^6 divine atoms, or 13,841,287,201 atoms of the divine plane combined together! The world we see around us is made of atoms, as we study in school, but the atoms of modern science are themselves made of many etheric atoms combined.

These combinations of atoms give rise to the seven planes of our solar system (Fig. 5).

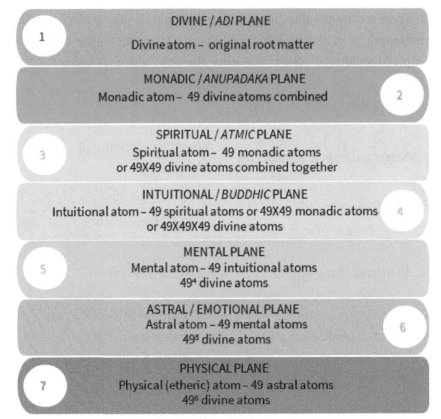

Fig. 5 The 7 planes of our solar system

What Are Planes?

We use the word 'planes' many times, sometimes we may say realms or worlds, e.g., astral world or mental realm. What are they, exactly?

Each plane is a place or a world where the soul exists and functions. For example, while we are awake, we are functioning in the physical plane (actually, we are aware of a portion of the physical plane, the part we can see; we are not aware of the invisible part of the physical plane, which is called the etheric part), however, when we sleep, our soul goes into the astral plane.

Before we were born into this physical body or after we die, the soul goes into the mental plane.

Planes are therefore different worlds where the soul exists. What happens in each plane, how they look, etc. are topics for a later time.

Sub-Planes

There are seven planes around us, each of which is made of 'atoms' of that plane. As we saw in the previous section, while many of the atoms combine (into groups of forty-nine) to create the atoms of the lower planes, many of the atoms remain as they are, without combining into bigger groups. These untouched atoms group together (similar to how atoms combine to form bigger structures called molecules in Chemistry) to form bigger combinations – e.g., seven atoms combined together, nineteen atoms combined together, etc. There will still be some atoms that remain without combining, but the rest will combine as described below.

Taking the physical plane as an example, we have the etheric atom which is the building block of all matter in the physical world.

Combinations of these atoms, for example, four or five atoms combined together, will form the building block of the second sub-plane of the physical plane, which is called the subatomic sub-plane.

Bigger combinations (for example ten or twelve atoms combined together) will become the building blocks of the third sub-plane, called the super-etheric sub-plane; even bigger combinations (eighteen or twenty[4] atoms combined together) form the building blocks of the fourth sub-plane, called the etheric sub-plane. Finally, even larger combinations form what we know as the gaseous, liquid, and solid states of matter around us (Fig. 6).

Our normal, waking consciousness is limited to the lowest three sub-planes of the physical plane – solid, liquid and gas. However, when we heal people, for example with Pranic Healing[5], we are working in the higher sub-planes – etheric, super-etheric, sub-atomic and atomic (and even in the astral and mental planes).

Similar to the process on the physical plane, the astral atom combines into larger and larger molecules, forming the seven sub-planes of the astral plane; this process occurs on all the seven planes.

This gives us the seven planes of our solar system, each of which is sub-divided into seven sub-planes, making a total of forty-nine sub-planes of our solar system (Fig. 7).

---

[4] The number of atoms that are indicated as combining to form the sub-planes is just an example to illustrate the concept. The reader should not take these number as being exact. However, the combination of atoms into groups of 49, 49^2, etc. to form the atoms of the lower planes, as described earlier, is exact.

[5] A no-touch, energy healing system developed by Grand Master Choa Kok Sui. For more information visit www.worldpranichealing.com or www.globalpranichealing.com

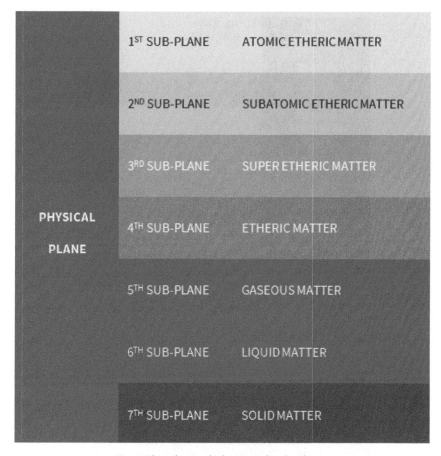

Fig. 6 The physical plane and sub-planes

Normal human life and evolution is limited to the three lowest planes (physical, astral, and mental) – these are the three worlds referred to in ancient Hindu texts – *bhur loka, bhuvar loka* and *svar loka*. However, as we evolve, we are able to function in the higher planes such as the intuitional and spiritual. The highest two planes, the monadic and divine are realms of manifestation of God.

DIVINE	1ST SUB-PLANE	
ADI PLANE	2ND SUB-PLANE	
	3RD SUB-PLANE	
	4TH SUB-PLANE	
	5TH SUB-PLANE	
	6TH SUB-PLANE	
	7TH SUB-PLANE	
MONADIC	1ST SUB-PLANE	
ANUPADAKA	2ND SUB-PLANE	
PLANE	3RD SUB-PLANE	
	4TH SUB-PLANE	
	5TH SUB-PLANE	
	6TH SUB-PLANE	
	7TH SUB-PLANE	
SPIRITUAL	1ST SUB-PLANE	
ATMIC PLANE	2ND SUB-PLANE	
	3RD SUB-PLANE	
	4TH SUB-PLANE	
	5TH SUB-PLANE	
	6TH SUB-PLANE	
	7TH SUB-PLANE	
INTUITIONAL	1ST SUB-PLANE	
BUDDHIC	2ND SUB-PLANE	
PLANE	3RD SUB-PLANE	
	4TH SUB-PLANE	
	5TH SUB-PLANE	
	6TH SUB-PLANE	
	7TH SUB-PLANE	
MENTAL	1ST SUB-PLANE	
PLANE	2ND SUB-PLANE	
	3RD SUB-PLANE	
	4TH SUB-PLANE	
	5TH SUB-PLANE	
	6TH SUB-PLANE	
	7TH SUB-PLANE	
ASTRAL	1ST SUB-PLANE	
PLANE	2ND SUB-PLANE	
	3RD SUB-PLANE	
	4TH SUB-PLANE	
	5TH SUB-PLANE	
	6TH SUB-PLANE	
	7TH SUB-PLANE	
PHYSICAL	1ST SUB-PLANE	ATOMIC
PLANE	2ND SUB-PLANE	SUBATOMIC
	3RD SUB-PLANE	SUPER ETHERIC
	4TH SUB-PLANE	ETHERIC
	5TH SUB-PLANE	GASEOUS
	6TH SUB-PLANE	LIQUID
	7TH SUB-PLANE	SOLID

Fig. 7 The 7 planes and 49 sub-planes of our solar system

> The three worlds or *lokas* are called *vyahritis* (literally meaning 'speech' or 'to utter'). The *sapta urdhvaloka* are the seven planes we have just studied – *bhur, bhuvar, svar, mahar, jana, tapar* and *satyam.*
> https://www.yogapedia.com/definition/10027/vyahriti
>
> Why are these worlds called *vyahritis*, which means 'to utter'? Because creation is based on the Word or sound, this is also why God is known as Logos (which means 'word' in Greek, as discussed earlier.)
>
> The *vyahritis* are also part of the Gayatri mantra.

Visualising The Planes

In many illustrations, the seven planes are shown stacked, one above the other. Due to this, there is a tendency to think of them as being 'above' us or 'below' us. In reality, the planes are all interpenetrating. They are right here, in and around us.

An example given by my teacher, Grand Master Choa Kok Sui, is a sponge immersed in water. Imagine the sponge represents the physical plane (for the moment, let us ignore the sub-planes) and the water represents the astral plane. The water is inside and outside the sponge. In the same way, astral matter interpenetrates physical matter; the astral plane interpenetrates the physical plane.

To take the example further, imagine we introduce a gas into the water – let the gas symbolise the mental plane. The gas is now inside the water and inside the sponge – the mental plane interpenetrates both the astral and physical planes.

Taking our planet, we have the physical Earth and the etheric Earth (made of matter of the four etheric sub-planes). The etheric part of the Earth is inside and outside the physical Earth (this is similar to the human aura, it is not outside the body, it is inside and outside the body).

Similarly, the astral body of the Earth interpenetrates the physical and etheric bodies and the same holds true for the other subtle bodies. They are all around us, inside and outside (Fig. 8).

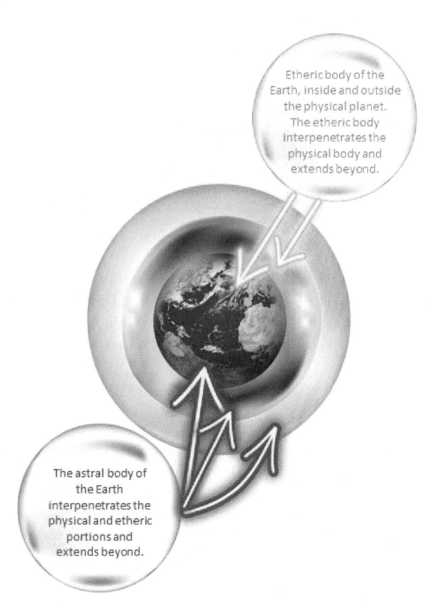

Etheric body of the Earth, inside and outside the physical planet. The etheric body interpenetrates the physical body and extends beyond.

The astral body of the Earth interpenetrates the physical and etheric portions and extends beyond.

Fig. 8 Etheric and astral bodies of the Earth

Chapter 2
The Second Life Wave

Once the seven planes and the forty-nine sub-planes have been created (and infused with the life of the Third Logos), the second outpouring or second life wave begins. This is the life or energy of the Second Logos (the love aspect, Vishnu, Allah Al Wadud or God the Son).

There are three separate, but related aspects to the second outpouring.

i.   The life of the Second Logos floods into all the seven planes and forty-nine sub-planes. The nature of the Second Logos is love, which is attractive and magnetic. Hence the effect of this life wave is to give matter the ability to combine into bigger and more complex forms, which will be suited to form the bodies of humans, animals, plants and minerals.

ii.   The second life wave brings in the *devas* or angels of our solar system, who also use the seven planes for their growth and evolution.

iii.   The second life wave brings in the divine sparks[6] that will incarnate and evolve in these planes.

Starting with the second point, there are many different types of angels of different levels of evolution, performing different functions.

Angels form a parallel evolutionary scheme, which is separate from the human evolutionary process. Yet, there is a lot of interaction and cooperation between humanity and the angelic kingdom.

One major difference, of course, is that angels do not have a physical body. Some may have an etheric body, others do not even have an etheric body, only an astral body, other angels may live in the higher planes.

Many of us think of angels as being very highly evolved. This is true, there are very highly evolved angels (e.g., the Archangels, Seraphim, Cherubim, etc.); however, like humans, there are angels at all levels of

---

[6] We will discuss the topic of divine sparks in Chapter 3, however, for the sake of some clarity, each of us is a soul, we are not just the body that is currently reading this book. What is a soul? The soul is our true self, that aspect of us which existed before this body was born and the self that will continue to exist after this body dies.

Think of this body as a vehicle, like a car, the soul is the driver. We may change from one car to another, but the driver is the same. Similarly, the soul may move from one body to another, but it is the same soul.

According to Theosophy, the soul manifests on three levels, which will be described further in later chapters – the ultimate self is called the divine spark. The manifestation of this divine spark in the middle planes is called the higher soul and the extension of the higher soul into the lower planes, including the physical body is called the incarnated soul.

evolution. Some may be less evolved than us, some are like us in terms of their level of evolution and others are very highly evolved.

Angels perform different functions. For example angels that heal, angels who help form our bodies after conception, angels of prosperity, angels of protection, etc.

A detailed study of the angelic kingdom will be a separate book in itself, so we will move onto the first effect of the second outpouring described above and then discuss the coming of the divine sparks in the next chapter.

The Three Elemental Kingdoms

The first effect of the second outpouring is the combining of matter (that has been formed by the first outpouring) into bigger and bigger groups or combinations. This is due to the quality of the Second Logos (the source of the second outpouring), which is love. Love is attractive, love is magnetic, it brings us together, it makes us want to be together.

In a similar way, the effect of the second outpouring flooding into matter is to give it this property to come together and combine into larger groupings of matter.

The second life wave (or second outpouring) is the life of the Second Logos flooding into the planes of our solar system, starting from above and flowing down[7] plane by plane until it reaches the mental plane. On each plane (and sub-plane), all matter is infused with the life of the Second Logos.

On the mental plane, all the atoms of the first mental sub-plane are infused with the life of the Second Logos. This infused matter is called monadic essence.

The life of the Second Logos also floods into matter of the remaining (second to seventh) mental sub-planes and this infused matter is called elemental essence.

The term monadic essence is only used for the atomic matter of the first sub-plane (infused with the life of the Second Logos), whereas the term elemental essence is used for the matter of the remaining six sub-planes (infused with the life of the Second Logos).

On the second and third mental sub-planes, the life of the Second Logos in the matter of these sub-planes (elemental essence) is called the first elemental kingdom.

On the other four (fourth to seventh) mental sub-planes, the life of the Second Logos in the matter of these sub-planes (elemental essence) is called the second elemental kingdom.

---

[7] We often use terms like 'flowing down into the planes', however, it helps to keep in mind the interpenetrating nature of the planes discussed in the previous chapter. The life wave does not really flow 'downwards', rather, it flows into the denser states of matter or into the denser planes.

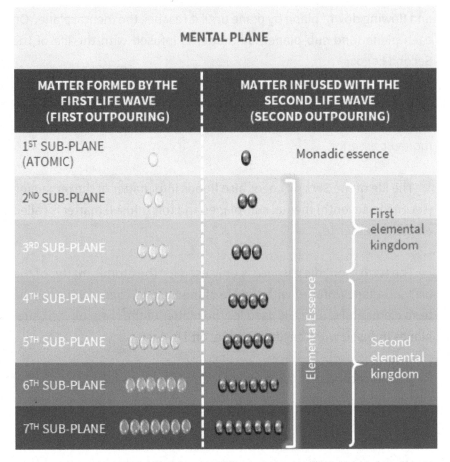

Fig. 9 Mental plane – monadic and elemental essence

In Fig. 9, matter on the left indicates matter of the seven mental sub-planes, formed by the first outpouring; on the right, matter is filled with the life of the Second Logos, indicated by the circles filled with colour.

For ease of illustration, matter of each sub-plane in Fig. 9 is shown with just a few atoms combined, e.g., on the seventh sub-plane, you see seven atoms combined. In reality, as explained in the previous chapter, the sub-planes are formed by bigger and bigger combinations of atoms;

matter of the second sub-plane could have four or five atoms combined, matter of the seventh sub-plane could have forty atoms combined.

> Why do we not speak of elemental kingdoms in the higher planes? According to C W Leadbeater, in the book *A Textbook of Theosophy*:
> "*The Divine Life pours itself into matter from above . . . The earliest level upon which its vehicles can be scientifically observed is the mental.*"

What is the difference between the elemental essence and the elemental kingdom? There is a subtle distinction between the two terms. When we say elemental essence, we are referring to matter, formed by combinations of atoms, filled with the life of the Second Logos.

When we say elemental kingdom, we are referring to the life wave coming from the Second Logos impregnated in the matter of these planes.

You could say, in a sense, that elemental essence refers to the matter or form, while elemental kingdom refers to the consciousness or life within the form.

Continuing with the flow into the lower planes, the life of the Second Logos floods into the atoms of the next lower plane, the astral plane, and here again, atomic matter of the first sub-plane, flooded with the life of the Second Logos is called monadic essence, while matter of the lower sub-planes (second to seventh) is called elemental essence. On the second to the seventh astral sub-planes, we have the third elemental kingdom (Fig. 10).

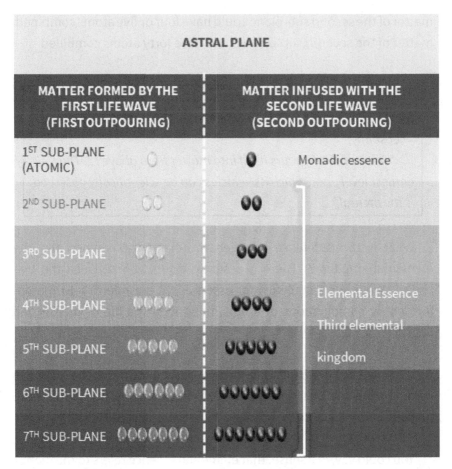

Fig. 10 Astral plane – monadic and elemental essence

Mineral Kingdom And Beyond

Having flooded matter of the mental and astral planes, the second life wave flows into the physical plane and floods the matter of the physical plane, first the etheric part of the physical plane, and then the visible physical part. Once again, the atomic matter of the first physical sub-plane, infused with the life of the Second Logos is called monadic essence.

However, the term elemental essence is not used for the matter of the remaining six physical sub-planes.

Having reached the lowest of the seven planes, the second life wave now changes direction and starts moving upwards again.

On the upward journey, the life wave floods into the vegetable kingdom, the animal kingdom and finally the human kingdom.

This gives us the seven Kingdoms of Nature as described in Theosophy:

1. First Elemental Kingdom
2. Second Elemental Kingdom
3. Third Elemental Kingdom
4. Mineral Kingdom
5. Vegetable Kingdom
6. Animal Kingdom
7. Human Kingdom

The three elemental kingdoms are on the downward arc of the second life wave, the mineral kingdom is the lowest point (at the mid-point between the downward and upward paths), and the final three kingdoms are on the upward arc.

The journey of the life wave from the first elemental kingdom downwards to the mineral kingdom is sometimes called involution, while the journey from the mineral kingdom upwards to the human kingdom is called evolution (Fig. 11).

We will discuss the mineral kingdom and other kingdoms in succeeding chapters when we study the journey of the divine sparks.

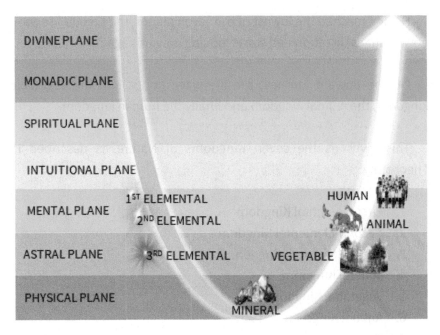

Fig. 11 The 7 kingdoms of nature

Chapter 3
The Second Life Wave
(The Divine Sparks)

The Divine Spark

We turn now to the second aspect of the second life wave (mentioned in the previous chapter), the bringing forth of the divine sparks.

Each of us is in reality, a divine spark. Our ultimate, true nature not only comes from God, we are a part of God. One example of this is to think of God as a fire, and each of us as a spark from that fire.

In several of the Upanishads, the self is referred to as *atman*. Two famous lines from the Upanishads (called *Mahavakyas* or 'Great Sayings') are:

Ayam atma Brahman – Brihadaranyaka Upanishad
"This self (*atma*) is *Brahman*."
(the Supreme Existence or Ultimate Reality)

Aham Brahmasmi – Brihadaranyaka Upanishad
"I am *Brahman*."

In the Bible, it is said,
    "So God created man in his own image,
    in the image of God he created him;
    male and female he created them."
    Genesis 1:27:

In the Quran:
    "Indeed we belong to Allah,
    and indeed to Him we will return."
    Quran 2:156

All these statements indicate the same truth, our true self (called the soul, divine spark, *atma* or other names) comes from God and is a part of God.

The divine sparks are 'made in the image of God' and hence, they manifest the three qualities of God that we discussed earlier – will, love and intelligence (also referred to as power, love and light).

The divine sparks are brought into the seven planes by the second life wave. They are not able to descend further than the monadic plane, they are too subtle to be able to manifest in what is the grosser matter (from their perspective) of the lower planes. However, as the second life wave flows into the lower planes, a portion of the divine sparks also descends into the three lower planes, the *atmic, buddhic* and mental planes.

You may ask, if a portion of the divine spark can descend into the lower planes, why can't the divine spark itself descend? This is a good question, and the answer given is that it is not really a portion of the divine spark that descends into the lower planes, rather, it is the rays of the divine spark that are able to 'shine forth' into the lower planes.

Think of the divine spark as being like the sun. The sun's rays reach us here on Earth and we receive the warmth, energy and life-giving properties of the sun. The sun itself is millions of miles away, but we benefit on the Earth through the sun's rays. In a similar manner, the divine spark itself remains on the monadic plane, but the divine spark 'shines forth' and sends its rays into the lower planes, carried by the second life wave.

The Spiritual Triad

The divine spark remains on the monadic plane. As it 'shines forth' into the lower planes, it is attached to one atom on each plane – one *atmic* atom, one *buddhic* atom and one mental atom (called a *manasic* atom)[8].

Through these three atoms and on these three planes, the divine spark will eventually be able to manifest its three qualities of will, love and intelligence. (Before this can happen, however, the divine spark has to descend into the lower planes, all the way to the physical plane and

---

[8] The actual attaching of the atoms to the divine spark is done by the *devas* or angels who are responsible for the task. The atoms are connected to the divine spark via the spiritual cord or *sutratma* (in Sanskrit).

then ascend through the planes again – this is described in the later chapters.)

The divine spark, manifesting on these three planes (*atmic*, *buddhic* and mental), through the three atoms is called the Heavenly Man, the Spiritual Triad, the higher soul or simply *atma-buddhi-manas* (Fig. 12).

The Spiritual Triad **is** the divine spark, it is not separate, but it is limited by the matter it has to work through. Imagine a person whose hands and legs are tied. It is the same person but limited by their circumstances. In the same way, the Spiritual Triad *is* the divine spark, but limited by the grosser matter of these planes (grosser from the perspective of the divine spark, but very subtle from our point of view in the physical body)

Another analogy may help – in our own homes, in our cities, we are familiar with the surroundings, we speak the language, we know our way around. We can say that we have our full capabilities. However, if we are dropped in the middle of another city in some other country, where we do not know anyone and where we do not know the language, we will be lost. We cannot communicate (assuming we do not have our mobiles phones with Google Translate with us!) and it will be difficult to find our way. However, over time, we will learn the local language, become familiar with the city and after some months or years, we will be as comfortable in that new city as we were in our original home.

In a similar manner, the divine spark is initially lost in the lower worlds and has to learn to live and function and manifest its potential in these lower planes. The journey continues until the divine spark can manifest itself, as fully as possible, in and through these lower planes.

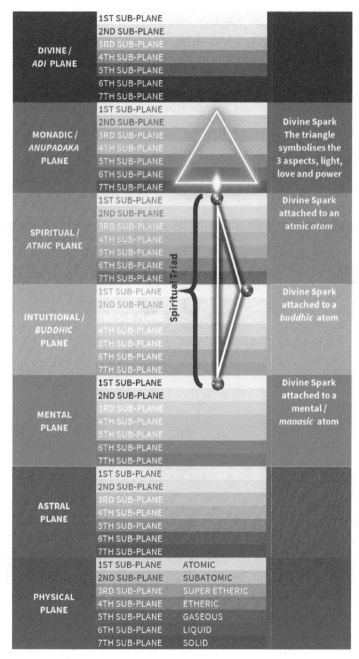

DIVINE / ***ADI* PLANE**	1ST SUB-PLANE 2ND SUB-PLANE 3RD SUB-PLANE 4TH SUB-PLANE 5TH SUB-PLANE 6TH SUB-PLANE 7TH SUB-PLANE	
MONADIC / ***ANUPADAKA* PLANE**	1ST SUB-PLANE 2ND SUB-PLANE 3RD SUB-PLANE 4TH SUB-PLANE 5TH SUB-PLANE 6TH SUB-PLANE 7TH SUB-PLANE	**Divine Spark** The triangle symbolises the 3 aspects, light, love and power
SPIRITUAL / ***ATMIC* PLANE**	1ST SUB-PLANE 2ND SUB-PLANE 3RD SUB-PLANE 4TH SUB-PLANE 5TH SUB-PLANE 6TH SUB-PLANE 7TH SUB-PLANE	**Divine Spark** attached to an atmic *atom*
INTUITIONAL / ***BUDDHIC* PLANE**	1ST SUB-PLANE 2ND SUB-PLANE 3RD SUB-PLANE 4TH SUB-PLANE 5TH SUB-PLANE 6TH SUB-PLANE 7TH SUB-PLANE	**Divine Spark** attached to a *buddhic* atom
MENTAL PLANE	1ST SUB-PLANE 2ND SUB-PLANE 3RD SUB-PLANE 4TH SUB-PLANE 5TH SUB-PLANE 6TH SUB-PLANE 7TH SUB-PLANE	**Divine Spark** attached to a mental / *manasic* atom
ASTRAL PLANE	1ST SUB-PLANE 2ND SUB-PLANE 3RD SUB-PLANE 4TH SUB-PLANE 5TH SUB-PLANE 6TH SUB-PLANE 7TH SUB-PLANE	
PHYSICAL PLANE	1ST SUB-PLANE 2ND SUB-PLANE 3RD SUB-PLANE 4TH SUB-PLANE 5TH SUB-PLANE 6TH SUB-PLANE 7TH SUB-PLANE	ATOMIC SUBATOMIC SUPER ETHERIC ETHERIC GASEOUS LIQUID SOLID

Fig. 12 The Spiritual Triad (*atma-buddhi-manas*)

To achieve this, the divine spark connects to one *atmic* atom, one *buddhic* atom and one *manasic* atom. As we saw in the previous chapter, the atoms of the mental plane, flooded with the second life wave is called monadic essence. To differentiate the atoms of the monadic essence from the atoms connected to divine sparks, the atoms connected to divine sparks are called permanent atoms.

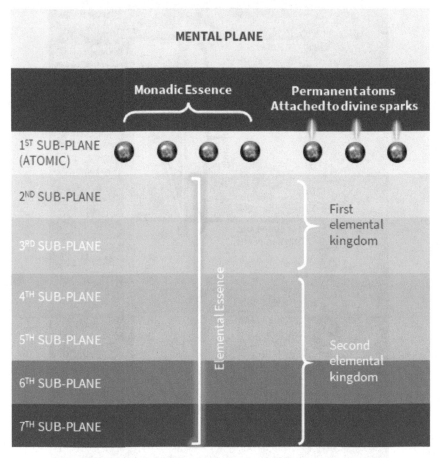

Fig. 13 Mental plane – permanent atoms (*manasic* atoms)

1) In Fig. 13, the circles represent atoms of the mental plane flooded with the life of the Second Logos. (The matter of the remaining sub-planes is not shown in this illustration.)

2) The unattached atoms constitute the monadic essence of the plane, the attached atoms are called permanent atoms (each permanent atom is connected to a different divine spark)

3) The matter of the lower sub-planes (second to seventh) flooded with the life of the Second Logos is called elemental essence.

4) On the second and third sub-planes we have the first elemental kingdom, on the remaining sub-planes (fourth to seventh), the second elemental kingdom.

The Lower Triad

The next step in the descent of the divine sparks into the seven planes is the formation of the lower triad (the lower counterpart of the Spiritual Triad).

As the life wave from the Second Logos flows down through the mental plane, on the fourth sub-plane of the mental plane, each divine spark (already connected to 3 atoms – one each on the *atmic, buddhic* and mental planes) is now attached to a molecule of matter on the fourth mental sub-plane. Grand Master Choa Kok Sui calls this the mental permanent seed, it is also known in some schools as the blue pearl.

Note the difference between the *manasic* permanent atom, which is an atom of the mental plane and part of the Spiritual Triad, and the mental permanent seed (which is not an atom, but a molecule of mental matter) on the fourth mental sub-plane and part of the lower triad.

The life of the Second Logos continues its downward journey and floods into the atoms of the next lower plane, the astral plane. Here again, each divine spark is attached to one atom of the astral plane.

As on the mental plane, these attached atoms are called permanent atoms, while the remaining atomic matter of the astral plane is called monadic essence.

Finally, the life wave from the Second Logos descends into the physical plane and each divine spark is attached to an etheric atom – once again, these attached atoms are called permanent atoms.

Thus, each divine spark is connected to six permanent atoms – one each on the *atmic, buddhic* and mental planes (the Spiritual Triad) and on the lower planes – one molecule on the mental fourth mental sub-plane and one atom each on the astral and physical planes (the lower triad).

The divine spark, manifesting through the three higher permanent atoms – *atma-buddhi-manas* is called the Spiritual Triad.

The Spiritual Triad (and thus the divine spark) manifesting through the three lower permanent atoms (mental, astral and physical) is called the incarnated soul (Fig. 14). (The term 'mental permanent atom is sometimes used, even though the particle is technically not an atom.)

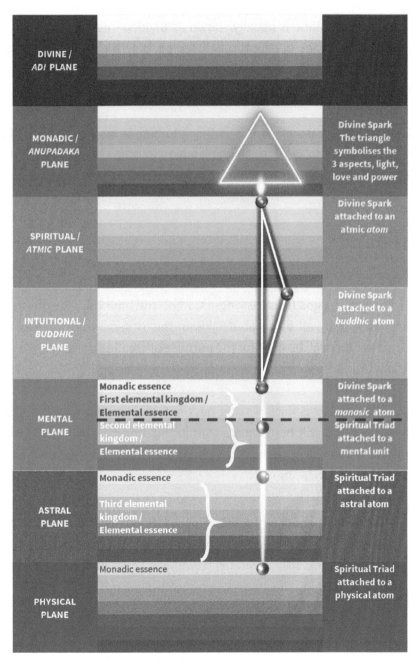

Fig. 14 The lower triad

The mental plane is usually shown as divided into two parts – the higher mental plane or causal plane[9] (comprising the first, second and third sub-planes) and the lower mental plane (comprising the fourth, fifth, sixth and seventh sub-planes).

One of the reasons for this is that the higher mental plane is the realm of manifestation of the higher soul or Spiritual Triad, whereas the lower mental plane is the realm of manifestation of the incarnated soul.

Summary

1. The Solar Logos fixes His ring-pass-not, the boundary for the solar system that will be created. Within this ring-pass-not is the root matter that will be used for the purpose of creating the seven planes of the solar system.

2. The Solar Logos fixes His ring-pass-not, the boundary for the solar system that will be created. Within this ring-pass-not is the root matter that will be used for the purpose of creating the seven planes of the solar system.

3. The creative aspect of the Solar Logos (Third Logos) sends forth His life wave (first outpouring) and combines the root matter (the ultimate atoms of our solar system) into combinations of 49, 49^2, 49^3, etc., forming the atoms of the lower planes.

---

[9] It is called the causal plane because our karma is stored here – the 'cause' of whatever we go through in life is found on this plane.

4. These atoms, on each plane, combine into groups or molecules forming the six lower sub-planes of each plane.

5. The love aspect of the Solar Logos (Second Logos) sends forth His life wave (second outpouring) which floods into all matter and gives matter the attractive power to form more complex combinations, these can be used to form the bodies of humans, animals, vegetables and minerals.

6. As the life of the Second Logos flows into the higher mental plane, it manifests as the first elemental kingdom, and on the lower mental plane, the second elemental kingdom.

7. On the astral plane, the second life wave manifests as the third elemental kingdom.

8. The life wave flows into the physical plane and the mineral kingdom and reaches the lowest point in the seven planes of our solar system.

9. The life wave then reverses and starts moving upward, into the vegetable, animal kingdoms and human kingdoms.

10. The second life wave also brings forth the divine sparks. These descend into the monadic plane and remain there. They are too subtle to be able to descend into the grosser matter of the lower planes.

11. A portion of the divine spark descends into the *atmic, buddhic* and higher mental planes, connecting to one atom on each plane. These atoms are called permanent atoms.

12. The divine spark manifesting through the *atmic, buddhic* and mental (*manasic*) atoms is called the Spiritual Triad or higher soul.

13. As the life wave flows into the lower planes, the Spiritual Triad connects to a molecule on fourth mental sub-plane, an astral atom and finally a physical atom.

14. These constitute the lower triad, the three lower permanent atoms through which the future incarnated soul will manifest on these lower planes.

15. Finally, the second life wave brings forth the devas or angels who inhabit different regions of the seven planes based on their level of evolution.

Chapter 4
The Permanent Atoms

The Seven Kingdoms of Nature

As we saw previously, the seven Kingdoms of Nature as per Theosophy are:

1. The First Elemental Kingdom
2. The Second Elemental Kingdom
3. The Third Elemental Kingdom
4. The Mineral Kingdom
5. The Vegetable Kingdom
6. The Animal Kingdom
7. The Human Kingdom

Each kingdom offers forms (or bodies) through which the divine sparks gain experience in certain planes and thereby grow.

Retracing our steps a bit, as the second life wave flows into the different planes, we reach the higher mental plane where the divine spark is attached to the *manasic* permanent atom. This completes the formation of the Spiritual Triad.

The next step is for the Spiritual Triad to connect to the mental unit (a molecule of mental matter on the fourth mental sub-plane). This mental unit (or mental permanent seed) is surrounded by elemental essence which constitutes the second elemental kingdom (on the fourth, fifth, sixth and seventh mental sub-planes).

Lower Mental World

The elemental essence surrounding the mental permanent seed is not fixed, it keeps changing[10]. The permanent seed finds itself embedded in and surrounded by different aggregations of elemental essence and through them, exposed to different vibrations.

The evolution of the permanent seeds (and therefore of the divine spark to which the permanent seeds are connected) is linked to the elemental kingdom, but the elemental kingdom is independent of the permanent seed.

Therefore, some aggregations of elemental essence may have in them one or more permanent seeds while other aggregations of elemental essence may not have any permanent seed in them.

---

[10] Elemental essence is many times more subtle than what we call a gaseous substance in the visible physical world. Just like a in gaseous substance, there is constant movement and flow.

Some of the elemental essence in which the permanent seed finds itself could be part of the body of an angelic being (just as our bodies are made of the matter of a particular plane, the bodies of the angels are made of the matter of a particular plane). As part of the body of an angelic being, the permanent seed will be exposed to a greater variety of vibrations.

As the permanent seed is exposed to different vibrations through the matter it is surrounded by, it develops the ability to respond to these vibrations, and the power to vibrate in certain ways, which will manifest later as the ability to form a mental body, the body which will serve as the vehicle used by the soul of a human to express thoughts.

> You may ask why we skipped the *manasic* permanent atom which is in the elemental essence of the first elemental kingdom as well as the *atmic* and *buddhic* permanent atoms. The reason is that the development of these atoms is linked to the evolution of the Spiritual Triad, which is part of the journey in the human kingdom.
>
> Hence, we can say that the divine spark, from the monadic plane, descends into the lower planes, manifesting as the Spiritual Triad, and the Spiritual Triad begins its journey with the descent into the lower mental plane as described above. The three lower permanent atoms are developed first and then the three higher permanent atoms.

Astral World

The entire process described above is repeated on the astral plane. The Spiritual Triad, connected to a mental unit, is now connected to an astral permanent atom, which is surrounded by the elemental essence of the third elemental kingdom.

As with the mental permanent seed, the astral permanent atom is exposed to different vibrations. It develops the ability to respond to those vibrations and acquires the power to vibrate in similar ways. This will manifest in the future as the ability to draw around itself astral matter to form an astral body – the body through which a human soul is able to feel or express emotions (hence another name for the emotional body is *kama rupa*, *kama* meaning desire in Sanskrit, and *rupa* meaning form.)

As in the mental world, some of the astral elemental essence may form part of the body of an angelic being, thus exposing the astral permanent atom to more varied vibrations.

Physical World

The next step is the development of the physical permanent atom. This happens in the mineral kingdom. The physical permanent atom is plunged into different materials and physical substances. The mineral kingdom is composed not only of solids, but also liquids, gases, and etheric substances.

Let us understand this process in a bit more detail, and it will help us also to understand how the process worked in the astral and mental planes in the earlier stages.

To quote Annie Besant from the book, *A Study in Consciousness*: *"A physical impact of any kind will cause vibrations . . . in the physical body it contacts . . . they will reach the permanent physical atom . . . This vibration, forced on the atom from outside, becomes a vibratory power in the atom - a tendency therein to repeat the vibration."*

What are these physical impacts and where do they originate from? For example, imagine a physical permanent atom which is in a rock deep in the Earth. It would experience the vibrations of heat and pressure that the rock it is embedded in experiences.

Imagine another physical permanent atom embedded in lava in a volcano, the vibrations it experiences will be totally different; another may be in the ice of Antarctica. In this way, by being immersed into different materials in different conditions of heat, depth, pressure, etc., the physical permanent atom is exposed to multiple vibrations, and it learns to respond to these vibrations and acquires the power to vibrate in similar ways.

The physical permanent atom is an etheric atom, six sub-planes more subtle than the physical (solid) rock it is embedded in. Nonetheless, each solid rock is surrounded by the different grades of etheric matter, and the physical permanent atom will be embedded in the etheric matter that interpenetrates the atoms or molecules making up the solid, physical rock.

Just as the physical permanent atom is exposed to many different vibrations and acquires the power to vibrate in similar ways, in the earlier stages, the astral and mental permanent atoms are similarly exposed to different vibrations on the astral and lower mental planes and acquire the power of those vibrations.

To quote Annie Besant from the same book,
"The use of the permanent atoms is to preserve within themselves, as vibratory powers, the results of all the experiences through which they have passed."

Summary

1) The second life wave flows into the planes, one by one, reaching the physical plane, and then reverses to go upwards, into the vegetable, animal and human kingdoms.

2) On the downward journey, we can think of the effect of the second life wave as being the grouping of matter into various combinations which show certain qualities, e.g., the ability to respond to thoughts or sensations (on the mental and astral planes), ending in the forms of the mineral kingdom.

3) On the upward journey which we will describe below, matter is ready to be formed into bodies – for the vegetable, animal and finally human kingdoms.

4) The permanent atoms of the divine sparks are exposed to the vibrations of their respective planes -

- o First the mental permanent seed on the lower mental plane (second elemental kingdom)
- o The astral permanent atom on the astral plane (third elemental kingdom)
- o The physical permanent atom on the physical plane (mineral kingdom)

Before we move on to study the journey of the divine sparks in the vegetable kingdom and other kingdoms, we need to discuss a few other topics.

Chapter 5
Group Souls

To understand the journey of the divine sparks beyond the mineral kingdom, we need to understand the concept of a group soul, and before that, the seven rays.

The Seven Rays

In the first chapter, we used the three primary colours (red, green and blue) to represent the three aspects of God. Taking this example further, by combining the three primary colours in various ways, we can create the seven colours of the rainbow.

When light is passed through a prism, we see the seven colours of the rainbow emerging from the other side. However, if we were to pass these seven colours through an inverted prism, they would once again merge into white light (Fig. 15).

Think of the white light as representing the energy of God. The three primary colours represent the three aspects of God that we discussed earlier – Will, Love and Active Intelligence. The seven colours of the rainbow symbolise the seven rays or seven primary qualities.

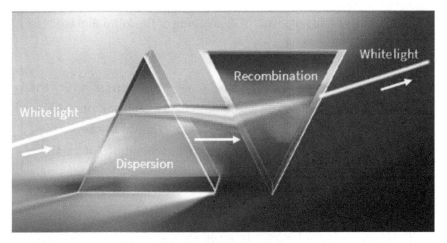

Fig. 15 Light passing through 2 prisms

As with the three aspects of God, the seven rays are not separate Gods, they are seven qualities or aspects of God as described below.

Ray 1   Will / Power
Ray 2   Love / Wisdom
Ray 3   Active Intelligence
Ray 4   Harmony / Beauty
Ray 5   Concrete Knowledge
Ray 6   Devotion
Ray 7   Ceremonial Magic

When the divine sparks are brought in by the second life wave, they are seen to belong to one of seven types corresponding to the seven rays, they denote seven different categories of divine sparks.

It is often asked why there are seven planes in our solar system and not more or less. The answer is that each plane is, in a sense, created by or connected to one of the seven rays. The seven chakras or the seven levels of awakening of the kundalini are also connected to the seven rays.

The seven notes of the musical scale, the seven colours of the rainbow, in fact, wherever we come across manifestation in seven varieties, we will be able to find a connection to the seven rays. These seven rays are in turn created by combinations of the three primary energies, will-love-intelligence, which are from the single source, God or Allah or *Brahman*.

Each divine spark belongs to a certain ray. Thus, we may speak of one particular divine spark as being a ray 1 divine spark whereas another would be a ray 3 divine spark.

When the divine sparks are brought in along with the second life wave, all seven categories of divine sparks are brought in at the same time.

Seven Rays in Matter

If spirit, represented here by divine sparks, belongs to one of seven types, it is seen that matter also belongs to one of seven types.

Just as *sat-chit-ananda* represent three aspects of *Brahman*, the three *gunas*[11] (qualities or attributes), *rajas, tamas* and *sattva* represent three aspects of matter.

> According to Grand Master Choa Kok Sui (in his book, *Inner Teachings of Hinduism Revealed*), the *rajasic guna* corresponds to will, *tamasic guna* corresponds to love and the *sattvic guna* corresponds to intelligence.

Once again, representing the three qualities of matter by the three primary colours, we can understand how they combine to form seven types of matter, corresponding to the seven rays.

Starting with the divine plane, we have seven types of divine atoms, corresponding to the seven rays.

In Fig. 16, the seven shapes represent seven types of divine atoms, each corresponding to a different ray. The sphere is a ray 1 divine atom, the cube is a ray 6 divine atom, and so on (the different shapes are for illustrative purposes only).

As discussed in Chapter 1, each of these atoms combines into groups of 49, 49^2, 49^3, etc. forming the atoms of the lower planes. However, we see that each plane has seven types of atoms corresponding to the seven rays.

---

[11] The concept of matter having three qualities or *gunas* is part of the *Samkhya* philosophy. Some of the earliest references to the *Samkhya* philosophy are found in the Bhagavad Gita.

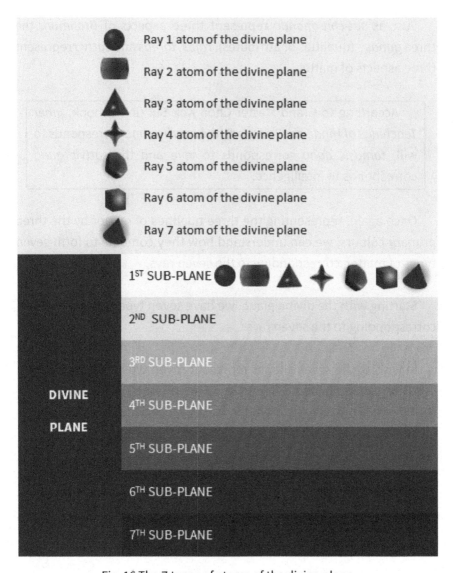

Fig. 16 The 7 types of atoms of the divine plane
(corresponding to the 7 rays)

On each plane, each type of atom combines to form molecules, creating the sub-planes. Every sub-plane, therefore, on each of the planes, contains seven types of matter corresponding to the seven rays.

In summary, the seven rays are the seven primary qualities of God and are the building blocks of everything we see around us, spirit and matter.

Group Souls

What is a group soul? As the name suggests, many souls grouped together or to be more specific, a collection of triads (three permanent atoms) grouped together is called a group soul.

When the Spiritual Triads are attached to a mental permanent seed (or blue pearl) on the fourth sub-plane of the mental plane, several such mental permanent seeds are enclosed in a sheath of matter forming a wall for the group soul. The wall is also composed of matter of the fourth mental sub-plane.

All the mental permanent seeds grouped together belong to the same ray, e.g., all ray 1 mental permanent seeds (a ray 1 mental permanent seed is a molecule of matter of the fourth mental sub-plane, which is formed by combinations of ray 1 mental atoms). However, these ray 1 permanent seeds are not necessarily connected to ray 1 divine sparks. They may be connected to divine sparks that are on any of the seven rays.

One ray 1 mental permanent seed may be connected to a ray 2 divine spark and another ray 1 mental permanent seed may be connected to a ray 5 divine spark. However, all the ray 1 mental permanent seeds are combined together in a group soul (Fig. 17).

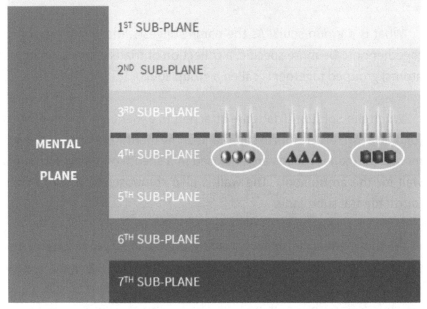

● Ray 1 mental permanent seeds (each connected to a different divine spark which may be of any ray), surrounded by matter of the 4th mental sub-plane, forming a group soul.

▲ Ray 3 mental permanent seeds surrounded by matter of the 4th mental sub-plane, forming a group soul.

■ Ray 6 mental permanent seeds surrounded by matter of the 4th mental sub-plane, forming a group soul.

MENTAL PLANE

1ST SUB-PLANE

2ND SUB-PLANE

3RD SUB-PLANE

4TH SUB-PLANE

5TH SUB-PLANE

6TH SUB-PLANE

7TH SUB-PLANE

Fig. 17 Mental plane – formation of group souls

Similarly, all ray 2 mental permanent seeds (permanent seed made of a molecule of matter on the fourth mental sub-plane, which is a combination of ray 2 mental atoms) and all ray 3 permanent seeds are grouped together.

All the mental permanent seeds grouped together are surrounded by the 'wall' of the group soul. This wall is also made of matter of the fourth mental sub-plane, and the molecules that make up the wall are of the same ray type as the mental permanent seeds within. A group soul containing ray 1 mental permanent seeds will have a wall made of ray 1 matter.

The next step, as we have seen earlier, is the attachment of an astral permanent atom to each mental permanent seed. The astral atom is selected from the same ray type as the mental atom that was connected earlier. In fact, all the six permanent atoms, the three permanent atoms of the Spiritual Triad and the three permanent atoms of the lower triad are selected from atoms of the same ray type.

Once again, the different groups of astral permanent atoms (belonging to different rays) will be surrounded and separated by a wall of astral atoms – the wall being made of astral atoms of the same ray type as the permanent atoms within.

The final step is the connection of a physical permanent atom to each astral permanent atom, and once again, the groups are surrounded by a wall of etheric atoms (of the same ray type). (Fig. 18)

Since we know that the different planes interpenetrate, the group souls can be better represented as indicated in Fig. 19.

The group of triads in Fig. 19 constitutes a group soul. Each of the triads has three permanent atoms (all belonging to the same ray) and each is connected to a divine spark, which may be on any of the rays. They are separated from other triads by the three walls of matter, one wall on each plane.

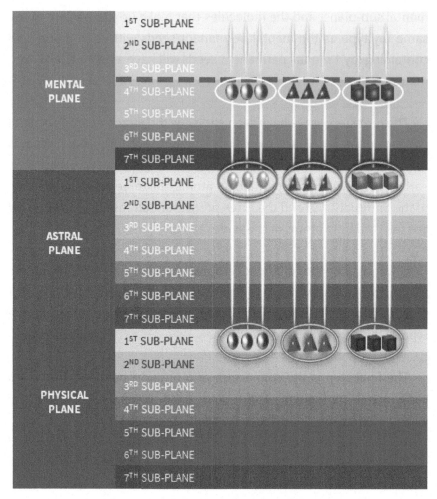

Fig. 18 Group souls – mineral kingdom

Not all ray 1 triads are combined together in one gigantic group soul, rather, there will be many ray 1 group souls, many ray 2 group souls and so on. As time passes, these group souls split, with fewer and fewer triads within them, until we reach the stage when each 'group soul' has only one triad in it.

This will be described later.

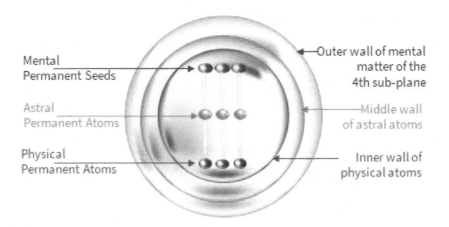

Mental
Permanent Seeds

Astral
Permanent Atoms

Physical
Permanent Atoms

Outer wall of mental
matter of the
4th sub-plane

Middle wall
of astral atoms

Inner wall of
physical atoms

Fig. 19 Group souls – mineral kingdom

We saw how the lower triad goes through different experiences on the different planes as part of the second life wave – the mental permanent seed on the lower mantal plane, through the second elemental kingdom; the astral permanent atom on the astral plane through the third elemental kingdom and finally the physical permanent atom on the physical plane through the mineral kingdom.

As part of a group soul, each permanent atom goes through different experiences (which reach the permanent atom as vibration as described earlier), but each atom also benefits from the vibrations experienced by the other permanent atoms in its group soul. The impact of the vibrations is the greatest on the permanent atom that directly experienced the vibration, e.g., the physical permanent atom embedded in volcanic rock, but the other permanent atoms in the group soul also experience the same vibrations to a lesser extent.

Thus, the group soul evolves through the experiences that each of the permanent atoms within it go through and the vibratory powers they develop.

Mineral Kingdom

Returning to our study of the journey of the lower triad in the mineral kingdom, not only does the physical permanent atom gain vibratory experience in the mineral kingdom, but there is also some stimulation of the astral permanent atom.

Elements exhibit 'attraction' for certain other elements or 'repulsion' from other elements; this is the beginning of the development of sensations or feelings, which exposes the astral permanent atom in the mineral kingdom to certain vibrations. This causes some astral matter to gather around the astral permanent atoms.

This astral matter is still a disorganised mass of matter, but it is the forerunner of what will be the future astral body of an animal and later still, a human being.

After a long period of time (usually one chain period – described in Chapter 8) some of the permanent atoms are ready to move into the vegetable kingdom.

Vegetable Kingdom

In the vegetable kingdom, the physical wall of the group soul, made of physical monadic essence dissolves and becomes part of the constituent matter inside the group soul, which now has only two walls – one made of astral atoms, and one made of fourth mental sub-plane matter (Fig. 20).

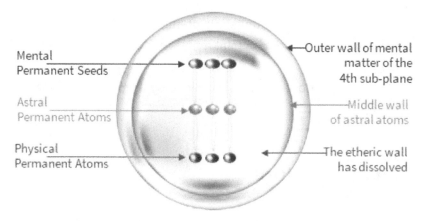

Mental Permanent Seeds

Astral Permanent Atoms

Physical Permanent Atoms

Outer wall of mental matter of the 4th sub-plane

Middle wall of astral atoms

The etheric wall has dissolved

Fig. 20 Group souls – vegetable kingdom

The three elemental kingdoms, the mineral kingdom, vegetable kingdom and even the lowest part of the animal kingdom seem to be independent of the evolution of the divine sparks. Not every blade of grass or every plant will have a permanent atom in it, though many may. We can think of the forms in these kingdoms as hosts, they 'host' the triads, but not as the bodies of the triads[12].

---

[12] In the human kingdom, the human body is created specifically for a human soul to inhabit, and when the soul leaves the body, the body dies. It is the same in the higher forms that belong to the animal kingdom. However, a blade of grass, for example, has its own existence and life, separate from the triads that may be in it.

As in the mineral kingdom, the permanent atoms are embedded in different forms in the vegetable kingdom, each exposed to different vibrations, both on the physical and astral levels. In the higher forms of the vegetable kingdom, for example in a tree, the astral atom gathers around it a more definite mass of astral matter, and through this 'astral body', begins to experience sensations such as pleasure and discomfort, caused, for example, by the weather, the temperature, and other factors.

There is also some stimulation of the mental permanent seed, manifesting as anticipation or faint memory.

After a long period, the triad is now ready to move into the animal kingdom.

Animal Kingdom

The atomic wall of astral matter dissolves into the matter of the group soul, which is now left with only one wall in the animal kingdom – composed of fourth sub-plane mental matter (Fig. 21).

In the lower forms of the animal kingdom, such as microbes, amoeba, etc., we may not always find a permanent atom (as described in the previous section, they act as hosts for the triads, they are not the bodies of the triads); however, the higher forms of animals will have a triad, each lion or each fox will have a triad within the body. This allows for further development of the three permanent atoms, including the mental permanent seed.

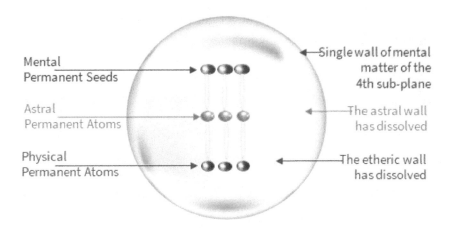

Fig. 21 Group souls – animal kingdom

There is an example given in Theosophy books to explain how the group soul functions. Imagine a group soul is represented by a bucket of water. As we have seen, within this group soul are many triads, and each triad may be in the body of a different lion, as an example. This can be equated to taking a mug of water from the bucket, and this mug of water is 'within' the lion and gaining experience through the lion – on the physical, astral and mental levels (Fig. 22a).

Let us equate this experience gained with the water taking on a certain colour, e.g., yellow. Another mug of water in a different lion may take on a pink tinge and yet another becomes blue (Fig. 22b).

When each of these lions die, the mugs of water are poured back into the bucket, which takes on all these colours, though watered down (Fig. 22c).

Taking this example further, once a mug of water is poured back into the bucket, we can never get the same mug of water again. In the same way, once a lion dies, we can never get the same 'soul' incarnating in another lion or in any other animal.

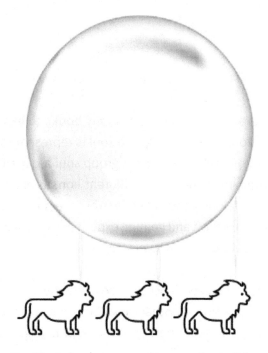

Fig. 22a Animal group soul incarnating in 3 lions

Fig. 22b Different colours, symbolising different experiences

Fig. 22c Group soul gaining from the experiences

Some readers may ask, "What about the permanent atoms? Can we not have one lower triad, occupying the body of a lion, and when the lion dies, the same triad goes into the body of another animal?"

This can happen and in fact, will happen, but we need to remember that the lower triads are not the soul, they are permanent atoms through which the soul can be embedded in various bodies to gain experience on those levels. Grand Master Choa Kok Sui says they are like plugs, they can be plugged into a body to fill the body with soul energy (life) and then unplugged to withdraw the soul energy (death).

Hence, even though same permanent atoms may go from one animal body to another, the 'soul' or 'consciousness' working through these permanent atoms is not the same.

Consider this example with a specific lower triad:

Life 1 – the three permanent atoms are in the body of a lion – Lion 1. They gain vibratory powers through the life of Lion 1. At the same time, the group soul that gives Lion 1 life is evolving – in our example of the mug and bucket, let us imagine that the initial mug of water representing the group soul was colourless, so Lion 1 starts with this 'colourless soul', however, by the end of the life of Lion 1, the soul is tinged yellow.

At the end of the life of Lion 1, the mug of yellowish water gets poured back into the group soul, along with other mugs of water from many other lions. The bucket of water that is the group soul now has many colours mixed together, from the many lives it has experienced, through many different lions.

Life 2 – the same set of permanent atoms that were in Lion 1, now enter Lion 2. However, the mug of water representing the group soul is no longer colourless, neither is it yellow. It has multiple colours. Hence the soul embodying Lion 2 is not the same as Lion 1, and in fact, is not the same as the soul in any previous lion.

The permanent atoms may be the same, but the soul / life / consciousness embodying the animal – through the permanent atoms – is never the same.

Division of Group Souls

As the groups souls evolve through the different kingdoms, they move to different forms in that kingdom, for example, moving from insects to lions and tigers, to cats, usually ending in domesticated animals. During this process, the groups souls keep splitting, leading to fewer and fewer triads in each group soul.

A group soul incarnating in lions, for example, may have hundreds of triads. As the group soul evolves, it splits and moves to occupy different bodies, e.g., bodies of cats, and it may now have ten triads within. Ultimately, there will be just one triad left in each 'group soul', as in the case of a domesticated cat.

> The seven types of divine sparks are embedded in different forms in the different kingdoms. For example, divine sparks of the sixth ray may be found in the canine family, wolves, foxes and culminating in dogs, while divine sparks of the fourth ray may be found in the feline family, lions, tigers, culminating in cats; second ray divine sparks end their journey in the animal kingdom in elephants.
>
> There are seven groups of animals, corresponding to the seven types of divine sparks, though ray 1 animals are not in existence at this time.

As the soul evolves through different animal bodies, something like a film appears within, separating one part of the group soul from another. In the example of our bucket, imagine a separator in the middle – water taken from the left side will go back to the left side and water taken from the right side will go back to the right side. Eventually, the two parts are so different that the group soul splits into two (Fig. 23).

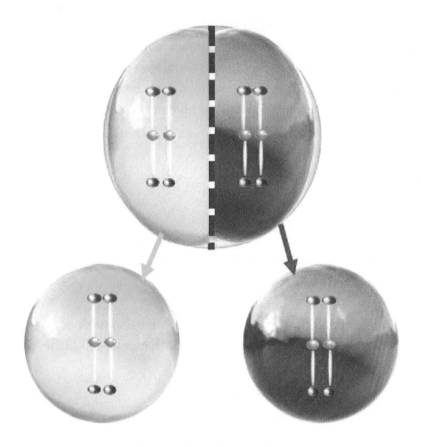

Fig. 23 Division of a group soul

This process continues until each 'group soul' contains only one lower triad. This is the point that we reach when we come to the end of the journey in the animal kingdom, in domesticated animals.

At this point, the group soul is ready to individualise and move into the human kingdom, though it may continue for several more lives in domesticated animals to better prepare itself for the journey in a human body.

For the triads, the journey through the six kingdoms leads to this final point before moving into the human kingdom, where each triad, alone in its group soul, having spent several lives occupying the form of a domesticated animal, is now ready to take the next step – individualisation and moving into the human kingdom.

The Journey So Far

1) The divine sparks connect to the three atoms that form the Spiritual Triad – one atom each on the *atmic*, *buddhic* and *mental* planes, often called *atma-buddhi-manas*.

2) The Spiritual Triad connects to the mental permanent seed (a molecule of mental matter) on the fourth mental sub-plane, which begins the formation of a group soul.

3) The mental permanent seed evolves through contact with the second elemental kingdom.

4) The astral permanent atom is then attached, this is the second step in the formation of the group soul. This atom evolves through exposure to vibrations in the third elemental kingdom.

5) Finally, the physical permanent atom is attached, the group soul is complete and is immersed in various forms in the mineral kingdom.

During the time in the mineral kingdom, the physical permanent atom evolves through the vibrations it is exposed to, additionally, but to a lesser extent, some vibrations also have an impact on the astral permanent atom.

6) The lower triad moves to the vegetable kingdom. The physical wall of the group soul dissolves, and the physical and astral atoms evolve through the forms they are immersed in. In the vegetable kingdom, there is also some evolution of the mental permanent seed.

7) The lower triad moves to the animal kingdom, where the astral wall of the group soul dissolves. All three atoms receive stimulation from life in various animal forms.

8) The group soul has been dividing all along, and now, in the animal kingdom, this division continues until there is only one triad of permanent atoms within a group soul envelop.

Eventually, this triad is ready to move into the human kingdom, a process called individualisation.

Chapter 6
The Human Kingdom

The Third Outpouring

Individualisation involves two aspects, the divine spark 'reaching down' and the group soul 'reaching up', both meeting on the higher mental plane (causal plane).

The 'reaching down' is called the third outpouring. This is the energy of the First Logos (the will aspect, Shiva, Allah Al Muqtadir or God the Father) flowing through the divine spark on the monadic plane, through the *atmic* plane to the intuitional (*buddhic*) plane and waiting there for the moment of individualisation.

The 'reaching up' aspect is the animal group soul, having reached the required state of evolution, moving up from the fourth mental sub-plane, where it is situated (which is part of the lower mental world), into the third mental sub-plane (which is part of the higher mental world).

This happens when the group soul wall made of matter of the fourth mental sub-plane dissolves or breaks up into smaller combinations of matter, thereby transforming into matter of the third sub-plane[13] (Fig. 24).

On the third mental sub-plane, the formation of the causal body allows the third outpouring, waiting on the intuitional plane, to flow into the causal body, forming the higher soul. The higher soul is the divine spark, manifesting as the Spiritual Triad, and now ensouling the causal body, using the causal body as its permanent 'home' through its journey in the human kingdom.

Thus, the animal group soul, which was on the fourth mental sub-plane, dissolves into the causal body on the third mental sub-plane. What was the soul (animal group soul) is now itself ensouled (by the divine spark as part of the third outpouring).

The third outpouring, unlike the first two outpourings, comes to each triad separately and individually, at the time of individualisation.

---

[13] All matter of the mental plane is made of combinations of the mental atoms. Matter of the fourth mental sub-plane is just larger and bigger combinations of mental atoms compared to matter of the third mental sub-plane. Hence, when matter of the fourth sub-plane breaks up into smaller combinations, it becomes matter of the third sub-plane.

The fourth sub-plane matter formed the group soul which guided the lower triads through the kingdoms, but now, it forms the causal body which is itself ensouled.

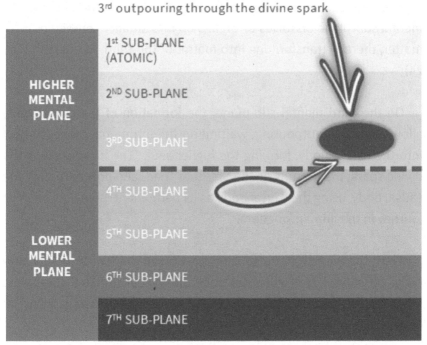

An animal group soul made of matter of the 4th mental sub-plane, dissolves into the causal body, made of matter of the 3rd mental sub-plane. The causal body is ensouled by 3rd outpouring flowing through the divine spark.

Fig. 24 Mental plane – formation of the causal body

> The soul of a human being is completely different from the group soul of an animal. Unlike an individualised human soul, an animal group soul has no causal body and has not received the third outpouring. Hence, once individualised, the human soul cannot return to the animal kingdom, or to put it another way, a human being cannot be reborn as an animal in a future life.

Summary of the Three Outpourings

1) The First Outpouring
   - Combines the ultimate root matter into combinations of 49, 49^2, 49^3 and so on up to 49^6 creating the atoms of the seven planes.
   - These atoms are of seven types on each plane, corresponding to the seven rays.
   - The atoms on each plane are further combined into larger groups, forming the sub-planes – there are seven types of matter on each of the sub-planes.
   - There are a total of seven planes, with seven sub-planes each.

2) The Second Outpouring
   - Due to the nature of the Second Logos which is love, infusing matter with the energy of the second outpouring causes matter to combine in even bigger groups, combinations that will be suitable to be used to form the bodies of the various kingdoms of nature.
   - The second outpouring brings in the divine sparks – seven types of divine sparks, corresponding to the seven rays.
   - The second outpouring brings in the angels who inhabit this solar system with us and who are on a parallel evolutionary journey.

3) The Third Outpouring
   - The third outpouring happens separately for each divine spark, at the moment of individualisation.

- The third outpouring, flowing through the divine spark reaches down to the higher mental plane, where it ensouls the causal body (formed by the mental wall of the animal group soul), creating the higher soul of a human being.

The Spiritual Anatomy Of A Human

We can now study the complete spiritual anatomy of a human being. Ultimately, each human being is a divine spark, residing on the monadic plane.

In order to grow and evolve, this divine spark descends into the lower planes, manifesting as the Spiritual Triad or *atma-buddhi-manas*. These three qualities are then ensouled in the causal body forming the higher soul (on the third sub-plane of the mental world).

The higher soul is connected to the three lower permanent atoms via the spiritual cord or *sutratma*. These atoms will enable the higher soul to form bodies on the lower planes (lower mental, astral and physical) through which it can incarnate and evolve (Fig. 25).

Incarnation

When the higher soul decides to incarnate, the first step is for the mental permanent seed to descend into the lower mental world, gathering around itself mental matter to form the lower mental body.

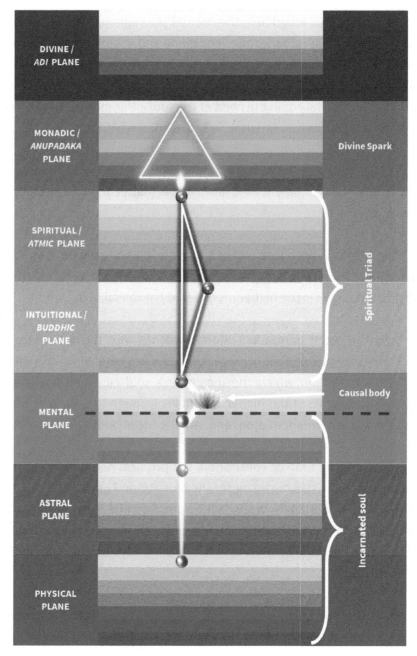

Fig. 25 Spiritual anatomy of a human being

In the previous kingdoms, the mental permanent seed developed the ability to respond to various vibrations and eventually to replicate those vibrations. That ability now allows the mental permanent seed to draw around itself mental matter (of the lower mental world) of different grades based on the need of the soul – this mental matter that is gathered becomes the mental body of a human being.

The life or energy of the higher soul flows through the spiritual cord into the mental permanent seed and into the matter of the mental body, giving it life.

This is the body or instrument through which the incarnating soul can think concrete thoughts (the body / instrument used to think abstract thoughts is the higher mental body or causal body).

Next the astral permanent atom descends into the astral world, gathering around itself astral matter to create the astral body, this is the instrument through which the incarnating soul can feel or express emotions. The life of the higher soul flows through the spiritual cord, into the astral permanent atom and into the astral body, giving it life.

Finally, at the time of conception, the physical permanent atom is connected to the sperm and egg of the parents, and once again, the life of the higher soul flows through the spiritual cord, into the physical permanent atom, giving life to the two cells. This begins the formation of the foetus and the beginning of the journey of the higher soul in the physical body.

As in the previous kingdoms, all the experiences that the human being passes through in that life, physical, emotional and mental, are stored as vibratory imprints and powers within the permanent atoms.

Death

When the soul has completed its journey in the physical form, the process is reversed. First, the physical permanent atom is 'unplugged' from the body. Without this connection to the higher soul, there is no life or soul energy in the body, and the body dies. The physical permanent atom is reabsorbed by the higher soul into the causal body.

The soul is now occupying the remaining two bodies, the lower mental and the astral. It continues to live in the astral world for a variable length of time, depending on the nature of life it lived when in the physical body.

Let us take the example of a person who struggled with an addiction to alcohol during their lifetime. When their physical body dies, the desire for alcohol does not disappear, in fact, it is felt even more strongly. This is because the astral body, in which the soul now resides, is the vehicle through which desires and addictions are experienced. However, there is no alcohol in the inner world.

This is what is referred to as "hell", as the soul is unable to satisfy its intense cravings, which are now many times more magnified than when in the physical body.

However, this 'hell' is not punishment by God or anyone else, it is the result of how we lived our lives and the effect of our life choices.

Slowly, the desire for the alcohol will die out, and the soul will be able to free itself from the astral world. If such strong desires are not present, the time spent in the astral world will be much shorter.

The question is asked, since the desire for alcohol (for example), dies out in the astral body before the soul can move on, why is it said that the person will be born with a desire for alcohol or a tendency to addiction in a future life?

The reason is that the soul has not really overcome its addition or desire by developing its qualities, of will power or discipline, for example. It was the circumstances of the astral world – specifically the lack of alcohol – that caused the desire to die out. The soul did not overcome the desire through its growth or evolution.

Hence, this task of developing the will or discipline or discernment to overcome addiction will need to be worked on in a future life.

After a period of time, the astral permanent atom is unplugged, and the astral body dies; the astral permanent atom is reabsorbed by the higher soul into the causal body.

The soul is now in its lower mental body where it reaps the benefits of all those thoughts and emotions that have been entirely unselfish. The life in the lower mental world is therefore happy and corresponds to what we call heaven.

However, neither heaven, nor hell is permanent. Eventually, the time in the lower mental world also comes to an end. The mental permanent seed is unplugged and the incarnated soul and the mental permanent seed are reabsorbed by the higher soul, into the causal body.

The entire process, from the initial 'descent' of the mental permanent seed into the lower mental plane, to the final reabsorption of the mental permanent seed back into the causal body is one incarnation from the perspective of the higher soul. According to some books, this can take between 800 years and 1,200 years, though in many instances, it can be much shorter. The time we spend in our physical body, what we think of as 'our entire life' can be just ten percent of one incarnation from the perspective of the higher soul.

Reincarnation

The life of the higher soul in the causal body varies based on the level of evolution of the soul. In the initial stages of the human journey, the higher soul is only partially conscious on the causal level (remember the example of being lost in a strange country, where we do not speak the language), but as the higher soul evolves through many incarnations, it has its own life and activities in the causal plane.

After some time, the higher soul feels the desire to incarnate again and the process of incarnation begins once more – with the formation of a new lower mental body[14], then astral body, etc.

The reason we do not remember our past lives, is that we require our lower mental body to remember things. Since we have a new set of

---

[14] The reader has seen in several instances the separation of the higher mental plane from the lower mental plane. The reason for this should be clearer now – the higher soul resides on the higher mental plane (also called the causal plane) while the incarnated soul begins its journey on the lower mental plane.

bodies for each incarnation, we do not have access to the memories of our previous incarnations. In each life, we (the incarnated soul) have a new set of lower mental, astral and physical bodies.

However, the higher mental or causal body has remained the same since we individualised – it grows and evolves through many incarnations, but it is the same causal body we began our human journey with.

Therefore, as the higher soul, in our causal body, we have a record of all our previous lives. This can sometimes filter down to the incarnated soul, as in the case of people who have visions or recollections of past lives.

> The author heard the story of a young boy who, between the ages of two and three, would correct his parents when they called him and say that his name was not what they were calling him, but a different name. The parents found this strange, as they did not belong to a tradition that believes in reincarnation.
>
> Some years later, when the boy was around seven years of age, the family visited a monastery in their country and the boy said the monastery was his home. The monastery had a record of all the previous priests who had lived there, and when the record was checked, there was a record of a priest who had lived in the monastery, with the name the boy had mentioned as being his name.

Karma

The law of karma is taught in all the religions, it is also called the law of cause and effect. In essence, it says that whatever we do (in our actions, words or thoughts), will come back to us, both good and bad.

Until we reach the human kingdom, we do not have individual karma because we do not have an individualised soul.

Why does one dog live a life of luxury, pampered by its owners, while another dog struggles to find food on the streets? It is the group soul of the animal that incarnates in various dogs, in different circumstances, in order to gain experience and grow. However, if a dog is hungry for example, it is not because in a previous life, it generated the karma to go hungry. There was no previous life of the dog, in the sense of a separate soul that goes from one dog to another, as we have seen in the previous chapter.

Once we individualise, however, we do have a separate soul and we also have free will (this is one of the effects of the third outpouring, which comes from the First Logos, the will aspect of God). The combination of free will and a separate, individualised soul brings every human being under the purview of the law of karma.

Our karma is stored in the causal body. This is why it is called the causal body, the 'causes' of whatever we go through in life are found in this body. In Sanskrit, the causal body is called the *kaarana sharira* (*kaarana* meaning cause and *sharira* meaning body).

When the higher soul decides to incarnate, it cannot arbitrarily choose where to incarnate, it is limited by its past karma and by the lessons it wants to learn in that life. Based on the lessons the soul wants to learn, and the circumstances it needs to learn those lessons, it needs to find a family which provides those circumstances.

For example, a soul needs to be born into a family of great wealth, but by the age of ten or twelve, needs to experience poverty. This could manifest as the soul bring born to rich parents (the soul would need to have the karmic connection with the parents to be born as their child, similarly the parents would need to have the karmic connection with the child to be the parents) and the family losing all their money some years later.

People may sometimes blame the child for bringing misfortune to the family. Or people may blame the parents for making wrong decisions that caused the family to become poor, causing the child to suffer.

In reality, it is the karma of all the people involved, parents and child, to go through these experiences. Our karma does not always have to manifest through our own actions, in this case, the child experiences poverty due to the decisions of the parents, however, it was the child's own personal karma that caused the child to be born into that family in the first place.

Whatever we are going through now is due to our past karma, however, the objective of karma is not to make us suffer, the objective is to help us learn and grow. Once we learn the lesson, the karma is neutralised.

What is the lesson of the child in the above example? There could be many possible lessons depending on the specific circumstances. Taking a negative example, perhaps the family lost their money because one of the parents was addicted to alcohol and gambling. The child, growing up in such an environment, may resolve never to drink or to gamble.

Another example could be the child, experiencing poverty, resolving to work and generate so much wealth, that money will never be a problem. The reader may ask, is making money truly a worthy objective for the soul? It is not the act of making money that is the key, it is how the soul goes about making money. In the process of working towards wealth, if the soul develops discipline, determination, intelligence and other qualities, it will be a life well lived from the perspective of soul. On the other hand, if the person starts lying, cheating and stealing to make money, it will not be a beneficial life for the soul.

Ultimately, it is how we live our life that is important. It is the lessons we learn through the challenges that we face, and how we learn and grow that makes the difference.

The law of karma is sometimes seen as fatalistic, but in reality, it is empowering. It gives us control of our life. If what we are going through is due to our past karma, then what we will go through in the future is based on how we live now. Our future is in our hands.

Chapter 7
The Human Journey

The higher soul is pure, but not yet perfect. What does this mean? We have studied the three aspects of the soul – light (or intelligence), love and power (or will).

Let us imagine that we can represent these three qualities by using different colours, e.g., green for light, red for love and blue for power.

When the higher soul achieves perfection, it will be represented as having all the three colours manifesting and combining to form white. That is the objective. However, as the higher soul is not yet perfect, it implies that some colours are missing.

Taking the analogy further, we know that there are many shades of red – crimson, ruby red, wine red, pink, etc. Each of these represents a different aspect of love, for example patience, forgiveness, understanding, etc.

In order to perfect the love aspect, the higher soul needs to develop all these shades of red (that is to say, to develop all these qualities of love). However, at our current stage of evolution, while some shades have been developed by the higher soul, others are still missing.

Fig. 26 Higher soul – love aspect incomplete

In Fig. 26, the missing shades represent qualities that the higher soul is yet to develop. Let us imagine that one of these missing shades corresponds to the quality of patience (as indicated). The higher soul, through its life and experience on the physical plane, needs to develop this quality; due to the lack of this and other qualities, the higher soul is not yet perfect. However, the higher soul is pure, so the absence of love does not manifest, at the higher soul level, as impatience, irritability, or anger, etc.

If our higher soul decides to acquire this quality of patience, for example, how would the conditions on the physical plane manifest to help us do this? We cannot magically develop patience, rather, we will be exposed to people and situations that will teach us (or sometimes almost force us) to develop patience.

If, through our life experiences, we develop patience, it will be symbolised as the missing shade of red appearing in the higher soul. If we fail to develop patience in that life and insist on behaving as impatiently as when we first began, not much progress is made.

Normally, however, when the soul decides to acquire a quality (whether patience or any other virtue), if we fail to make use of the opportunities presented by the circumstances of our life, the challenges we face will keep increasing, almost forcing us to learn the lesson.

In this way, lifetime after lifetime, the higher soul incarnates with the objective of developing different qualities. Based on the qualities we wish to develop, and based on our previous karma, we incarnate at certain times, in certain places, in a certain race and to a certain family, etc.

As we learn our lessons in life and develop various qualities, those qualities or 'colours' are filled in at the higher soul level (Fig. 27).

Ultimately, when we have developed all the qualities of light, love and power, the higher soul becomes perfect and merges with the divine spark. This is *moksha* (or liberation) as described in Indian texts – the higher soul has worked out all its karma, it has learnt all its lessons, it does not need to incarnate anymore.

Fig. 27 Higher soul – love aspect perfected

Initiations

As the soul develops more and more qualities, it progresses on its journey towards perfection and along the way, certain stages are marked by what are referred to as initiations.

We can think of initiations as events in the inner world, similar to graduation ceremonies, signifying a level of achievement that the soul has attained. When we graduate from school, for example, it is an acknowledgement of having learnt and understood specific lessons and of having passed the required examinations. Graduation from school also entitles us to move on to college, similarly, initiation gives the soul access to the next stage of growth and higher teachings.

As the higher soul grows through successive incarnations, we reach a point where the higher soul attains the first initiation.

This happens when the soul has developed substantial control over the physical body. The key word is 'substantial'. It is necessarily vague – hence one person may be very disciplined when it comes to waking up and exercising, but struggles with controlling their diet, while another may be the exact opposite, they are very disciplined with eating, but can't get themselves to wake up and exercise.

In the Buddhist teachings, a person whose soul has taken the first initiation is called a *sotapanna* which means, 'one who has entered the stream'.

After several more lives, the soul takes the second initiation, this is when there is substantial control over the emotions. The Buddhist term for such a person is *sakadagamin* (he who returns once – referring to the belief that after achieving this initiation, the soul needs just one more incarnation to achieve union – this is described further below).

The third initiation occurs when the soul has substantially controlled the thoughts. Such a person is called an *anagamin*[15] in Buddhism (meaning he who does not return, referring to the belief that third initiate will achieve union with the higher soul in that same life and will not need to incarnate again, unless they choose to).

---

[15] In Indian texts, the term for a *anagamin* is *hamsa*. *Hamsa* refers to a swan or goose or sometimes it is said to be a mythical bird that is capable of separating milk from water, symbolising the ability of a person who has reached this level of spiritual growth to discern reality from what is unreal.

The fourth initiation is when the incarnated soul becomes one with the higher soul – this is yoga or union and the person is called an *arhat* ('one who is worthy') or in other traditions, *Paramahamsa, Lohan, Arihant* or a Saint.

The fifth initiation is when the higher soul, having become perfect (which means all the three qualities of light, love and power have been perfected as described earlier – perfected from the human perspective), merges with the divine spark.

Such a person is called an *asheka* ˛ an adept or a Holy Master. This is when we achieve *moksha*, we do not need to incarnate again, because we have learnt all that there is to learn in this physical realm. The divine spark has not only learnt to function in the lower planes, it has mastered the lower planes. We have worked out all our karmas, we have become perfect, "even as your Father, which is in heaven, is perfect." Matthew 5:48

After the fifth initiation, the soul continues to evolve, the sixth initiate is called a *Chohan*, the seventh initiate is called a *Bodhisattva* and the eighth initiate is called a *Buddha*.

There are higher initiations, but of these, not much is written or known.

Until we reach the level of a fourth initiate, an *arhat*, we are told that incarnation is not an option, the soul has to incarnate in order to work out its karma and evolve.

Once we become an *arhat*, we do have a choice. We can continue to grow and learn by incarnating, or without taking a physical body. However, most *arhats* do choose to incarnate, because by doing so, they are able to help, guide, teach and inspire many people – think of the impact of great teachers like Paramahamsa Yogananda, Ramakrishna Paramahamsa, Mother Teresa, Grand Master Choa Kok Sui, and many others.

Once the fifth initiation is achieved, there are no further incarnations needed as there is nothing left for the soul to learn in this physical realm. However, some teachers at this level may incarnate from time to time, to guide humanity. One such Holy Master, according to Grand Master Choa Kok Sui, is Sri Yukteshwar Giri, Paramahamsa Yogananda's teacher. Another is Holy Master Djwal Khul, who guided Alice Bailey.

More About Yoga

When we talk about achieving union, what does that mean exactly? What does it mean when we say that the incarnated soul becomes one with the higher soul? Are they not already one?

This is one of the questions that comes up in the different schools of *Vedanta* such as *Advaita* and *Dvaita*. The *Dvaita* (meaning duality) philosophy says that the soul and God are separate, whereas the *Advaita* (non-duality) philosophy says they are one.

As we have seen in previous chapters, the incarnated soul is not only connected to the higher soul, it is a part of the higher soul – a portion of the higher soul that descends into this body. Therefore, what is mean by 'becoming one with the higher soul?'

Take our internet connection as an example. If you went online thirty years ago, with a dial-up connection, you would have experienced how slow and unreliable the connection was. Downloading even a small file could take a long time, sometimes the notification would say that the download will complete in 6 months, 7 days, 5 hours, etc!! If we received a phone call, the internet connection was cut.

Our connection to our higher soul is similar, we are connected, but the connection is not very reliable, and the communication is minimal.

As we grow spiritually, the connection gets enhanced, eventually, it will be like having a fibre optic cable between the incarnated soul and higher soul – the connection is so fast and reliable, that the two *act* or *function* as one. This is what is meant by yoga or union.

Yoga is not just the theoretical oneness that is already present, but an experienced oneness which is what we are working towards.

Hence, Grand Master Choa Kok Sui states that the *Advaita* school describes the ultimate reality of oneness, while the *Dvaita* school describes our current, practical experience of separation and duality.

Achieving Yoga

The key to spiritual development is character building. How we live our life, what we do, what we say, how we feel and what we think; in all situations, with every person and being, including ourselves, at all times, this is what is critical to spiritual growth.

Meditation helps and is extremely beneficial, but meditation alone, without character building does not work.

To quote Grand Master Choa Kok Sui:
*"If a spiritual practitioner does not purify thoroughly,
the negative qualities and weaknesses will come back to haunt the
disciple. This will manifest as a spiritual fall."*
                    Beyond The Mind, Golden Lotus Sutra on Meditation

This is not a new teaching. In the Lord Buddha's Eightfold Noble Path, the way to Buddhahood begins with:
i.   Right Viewpoint
ii.   Right Thoughts
iii.   Right Speech
iv.   Right Actions

In the Zoroastrian religion, one of the main teachings is to practice good thoughts, good words and good deeds *(Humata, Hūxta, Huvarshta)*.

In the Old Testament, many of the Ten Commandments focused on how we should behave:

Honour your father and your mother.
Thou shalt not kill.
Thou shalt not steal.

In the New Testament, in the Sermon on the Mount, the Lord Jesus emphasises the behaviour of a spiritual disciple.

In the Yoga Sutras of Patanjali, the *ashtanga-yoga* begins with *yama* (things to avoid) and *niyama* (things to do), which is essentially character building.

Character building is an important part of the teachings of Islam. The Holy Koran has numerous examples of this.

A man once asked, "What admits most people into Paradise?"
The Prophet (peace be upon him) replied,
"Mindfulness of Allah (*al-taqwa*) and good character."
(Al-Bukhari, 1422 AH)

These teachings are not new, it is how we behave, how we treat one another and how we treat ourselves that form the foundation of spiritual growth.

Acts of charity, making donations, doing service, etc., become natural expressions of the change in our character. When we build on this foundation with meditation, our spiritual growth is accelerated.

Finally, as important as character building and meditation are on the spiritual path, the essential requirement is God's blessings.

Chapter 8
Rounds And Chains

One final topic will complete this introduction to the teachings of Theosophy.

We are told that before our recorded history, there was an ancient and advanced civilisation known as the Atlantean race. Before that was an earlier and more ancient civilisation called the Lemurian race and before Lemuria were older civilizations called the Hyperborean race and Polar race. In Theosophy, each of these civilisations is called a root race.

First root race	Polar
Second root race	Hyperborean
Third root race	Lemurian
Fourth root race	Atlantean
Fifth root race	Aryan (our current root race)
Sixth root race	In the future
Seventh root race	In the future

We are thus in the fifth root race, called the Aryan race and we are told that there will be two more root races to come.

The total of these seven root races comprises the time spent on our planet Earth, and this is called one world period.

1 world period = 7 root races

Before the first root race on Earth, we are told that life existed and evolved on another planet (Mars). Similarly, after the seventh root race on Earth, we are told that life will move to, and continue evolving on Mercury. In total, there are seven planets (including the Earth) on which life evolves, one by one. On each planet, life spends one world period (time equivalent to seven root races).

In the Fig. 28, the seven globes represent the seven planets on which life evolves, one by one. The yellow globe represents the first planet on which life evolves – on this planet life spends one world period, which is equivalent to seven root races.

Life then moves to the second planet, where it spends one world period (once again equivalent to seven root races), then moves on to the third planet, and so on, until it reaches the seventh and final planet. On each planet, life goes through seven root races. The total time spent on the seven planets (seven root races per planet) is called one round (Fig. 29).

1 round = 7 world periods = 49 root races

This entire process, when repeated seven times, that is, seven rounds, is called one chain. Therefore, in one chain, life goes through each of the seven planets, seven times – a total of forty-nine world periods. Since each world period has seven root races, we have:

1 chain = 7 rounds = 49 world periods = 343 root races

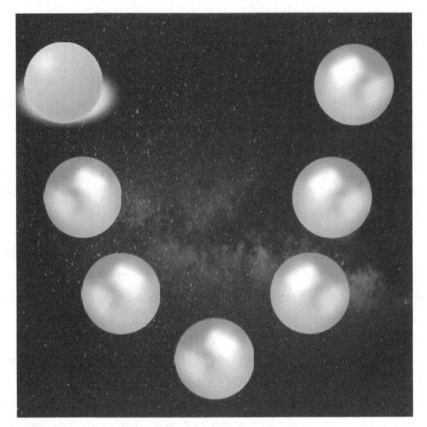

Fig. 28 First world period

Theosophy also teaches us that before the current set of seven planets, life evolved on a totally different set of seven planets and there were three such sets (each with seven planets). Similarly, after we complete our evolution on the current set of seven planets, we will move to another set of seven planets and there will be three more such sets.

Therefore, in total, there are seven sets of seven planets each. Let us consider them one by one.

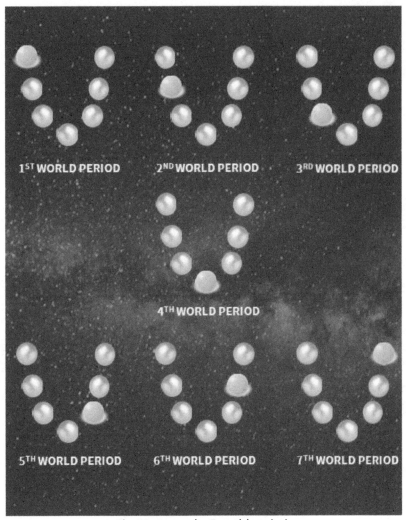

Fig. 29 1 round = 7 world periods

First Chain

The first set of seven planets is used by life in the first chain. As you can see below and in Fig. 30, these planets were not on the physical plane, they were planets that were composed of the matter of the subtler planes.

2 planets   1A and 1G that were on the spiritual plane
2 planets   1B and 1F that were on the intuitional plane
2 planets   1C and 1E that were on the higher mental plane
1 planet   1D that was on the lower mental plane

As described earlier, life moved through each of these planets, going through seven root races on each planet (called one world period). The total time spent on all seven planets (seven world periods) is called one round, and the repetition of this seven times (seven rounds) is called one chain.

On completion of the first chain, life moves on to another set of seven planets. This is like our soul, completing its journey in our bodies (physical, astral and mental), then leaving the bodies, to move on to a different set of bodies in the next incarnation.

What happens to the human bodies that have been discarded? They disintegrate and return to their original state. Similarly, the 'bodies' of the planets that have been utilised eventually disintegrate.

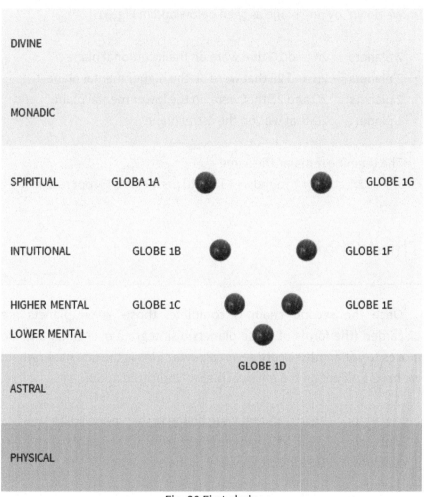

DIVINE

MONADIC

SPIRITUAL   GLOBA 1A   GLOBE 1G

INTUITIONAL   GLOBE 1B   GLOBE 1F

HIGHER MENTAL   GLOBE 1C   GLOBE 1E

LOWER MENTAL

                                    GLOBE 1D

ASTRAL

PHYSICAL

Fig. 30 First chain

Second Chain

The second chain is composed of a new set of seven planets, but they 'move down' by one plane as seen below and in Fig. 31.

2 planets   2A and 2G that were on the intuitional plane
2 planets   2B and 2F that were on the higher mental plane
2 planets   2C and 2E that were on the lower mental plane
1 planet   2D that was on the astral plane

The timeline remains the same –
2nd chain = 7 rounds = 49 world periods = 343 root races

Third Chain

Once the second chain is complete, those seven planets are discarded (the forms of those planets disintegrate over time) and life moves to yet another set of seven planets. This is the first chain where we have a planet on the physical plane – indicated as 3D.

2 planets   3A and 3G that were on the higher mental plane
2 planets   3B and 3F that were on the lower mental plane
2 planets   3C and 3E that were on the astral plane
1 planet   3D that was on the physical plane

Once again, the forms of these planets disintegrate when life moves to the fourth chain. The remnant of the physical planet (3D) is what we call our moon (Fig. 32). For this reason, the third chain is also sometimes called the moon chain.

Fourth Chain

The fourth chain continues the process of moving down one plane and there are three planets in the physical plane.

2 planets	4A and 4G on the lower mental plane
2 planets	4B and 4F the astral plane
3 planets	4C, 4D and 4E on the physical plane

We are currently in the fourth chain (also called the Earth chain) and the planets 4C, 4D and 4E correspond to Mars, Earth and Mercury respectively. There are no names given to the other four planets of our chain because they are not in the physical plane (Fig. 33).

Fifth Chain

Perhaps you have come across the phrase, "As above, so below."[16] We see here an example of that statement. Just as the second life wave (or second outpouring) flows 'down' into the physical plane, then retraces to move upwards (as it goes through the seven Kingdoms of Nature), the movement of the planets in the fifth chain and succeeding

---

[16] "As above, so below; as below, so above," is said to be a Hermetic axiom, quoted in the book, The Kybalion.

chains, having moved to the lowest point in the fourth chain, starts moving upwards[17].

Hence, in the fifth chain, there is only one physical planet, similar to the third chain. These planets have not been created yet; they are far in the future (Fig. 34).

2 planets	5A and 5G will be on the higher mental plane
2 planets	5B and 5F will be on the lower mental plane
2 planets	5C and 5E will be on the astral plane
1 planet	5D will be on the physical plane

Sixth Chain

The planets of this chain will be on the same planes as the planets of our second chain (Fig. 35).

2 planets	6A and 6G will be on the intuitional plane
2 planets	6B and 6F will be on the higher mental plane
2 planets	6C and 6E will be on the lower mental plane
1 planet	6D will be on the astral plane

---

[17] Another example is the journey of the higher soul. It moves 'down' when incarnating to inhabit a physical body, and when the body dies, it moves 'up' to return to its dwelling place on the higher mental world.

Seventh Chain

The seventh Chain will be similar to the first chain (Fig. 36).

2 planets	7A and 7G will be on the spiritual plane
2 planets	7B and 7F will be on the intuitional plane
2 planets	7C and 7E will be on the higher mental plane
1 planet	7D will be on the lower mental plane

The planets of the fifth, sixth and seventh chains are far in the future (millions of years) and they have not been formed yet.

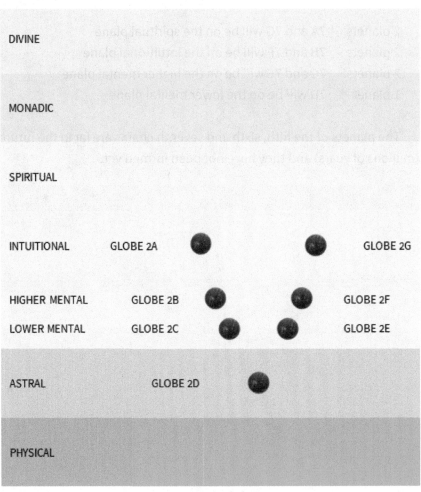

Fig. 31 Second chain

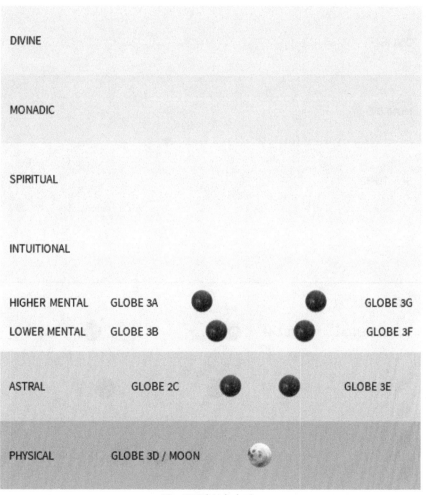

Fig. 32 Third chain

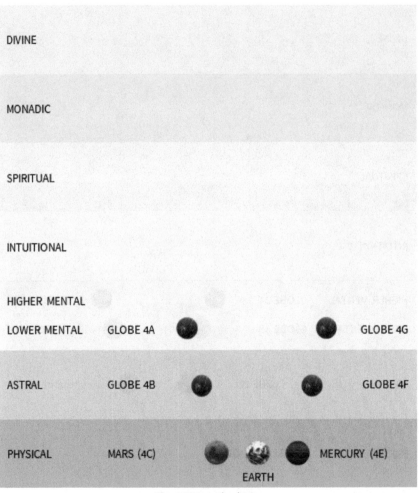

DIVINE

MONADIC

SPIRITUAL

INTUITIONAL

HIGHER MENTAL

LOWER MENTAL   GLOBE 4A   GLOBE 4G

ASTRAL   GLOBE 4B   GLOBE 4F

PHYSICAL   MARS (4C)   MERCURY (4E)
                              EARTH

Fig. 33 Fourth chain

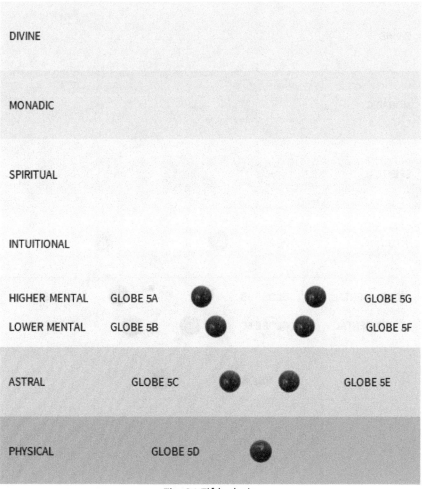

DIVINE

MONADIC

SPIRITUAL

INTUITIONAL

HIGHER MENTAL   GLOBE 5A   GLOBE 5G

LOWER MENTAL   GLOBE 5B   GLOBE 5F

ASTRAL   GLOBE 5C   GLOBE 5E

PHYSICAL   GLOBE 5D

Fig. 34 Fifth chain

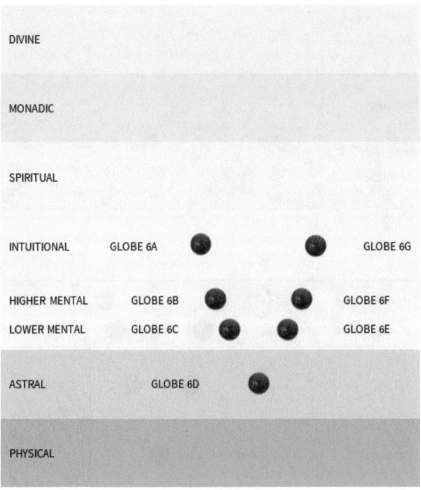

Fig. 35 Sixth chain

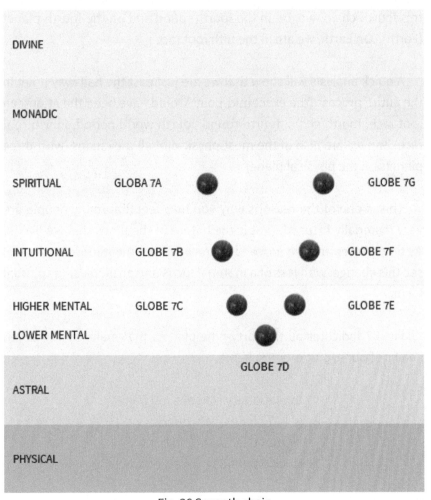

DIVINE

MONADIC

SPIRITUAL   GLOBA 7A   GLOBE 7G

INTUITIONAL   GLOBE 7B   GLOBE 7F

HIGHER MENTAL   GLOBE 7C   GLOBE 7E

LOWER MENTAL

                              GLOBE 7D

ASTRAL

PHYSICAL

Fig. 36 Seventh chain

Where Are We Now?

We are currently in the fourth chain, with three physical planets. In this fourth chain, we are in the fourth round and on the fourth planet (Earth). On Earth, we are in the fifth root race.

A quick analysis will show that we are just past the half-way point in the entire process (the exact mid-point would have been the Atlantean root race, fourth chain, fourth round, fourth world period, fourth root race) and we are also in the most physical of all the chains (with three planets on the physical plane).

This is one of the reasons why you may feel that many people are very materially focused; that is the nature of the times that we live in. As time passes and we move further away from the mid-point, we will see this change, with less of a material focus and an increasing spiritual focus.

Fig. 37 indicates all the forty-nine planets that make up the seven chains of our evolutionary scheme.

1 evolutionary scheme = 7 chains
7 chains = 49 rounds
49 rounds = 343 world periods
343 world periods = 2,401 root races

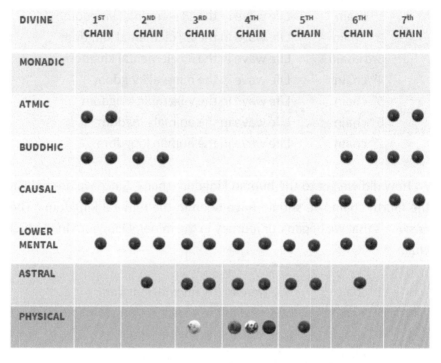

DIVINE	1ST CHAIN	2ND CHAIN	3RD CHAIN	4TH CHAIN	5TH CHAIN	6TH CHAIN	7th CHAIN
MONADIC							
ATMIC	● ●						● ●
BUDDHIC	● ●	● ●				● ●	● ●
CAUSAL	● ●	● ●	● ●		● ●	● ●	● ●
LOWER MENTAL	●	● ●	● ●	● ●	● ●	● ●	●
ASTRAL		●	● ●	● ●	● ●	● ●	●
PHYSICAL			●	● ● ●	●		

Fig. 37 The seven chains of our planetary scheme

Progress Through The Chains

In previous chapters we studied the evolution of the second life wave, passing through one kingdom of nature, before moving to the next one. The time that the life wave spends in each kingdom is one chain-period. Therefore, the permanent atoms that are today in the mineral kingdom would have been in the third elemental kingdom in the previous chain (the third chain or Moon chain). These permanent atoms would have been in the second elemental kingdom in the second chain and in the first elemental kingdom prior to that.

111

1st chain	Life wave in the 1st elemental kingdom
2nd chain	Life wave in the 2nd elemental kingdom
3rd chain	Life wave in the 3rd elemental kingdom
4th chain	Life wave in the mineral kingdom
5th chain	Life wave in the vegetable kingdom
6th chain	Life wave in the animal kingdom
7th chain	Life wave in the human kingdom

How did we get to the human kingdom then? Since we are only in the fourth chain, we should have been in the mineral kingdom. The answer is that we began our journey in the mineral kingdom in the first chain.

1st chain	We were in the mineral kingdom
2nd chain	We were in the vegetable kingdom
3rd chain	We were in the animal kingdom
4th chain	We are in the human kingdom

What about the three elemental kingdoms? Why did we not pass through them? The answer is we did, in the previous solar system! Here we see another example of the phrase, "As above, so below."

Just as we move from body to body, just as the life wave moves from planet to planet (and from chain to chain), similarly, the life of the Solar Logos moves from one solar system to another. Our previous 'incarnations' in the elemental kingdoms would have been in the previous 'incarnation' of our solar system. Since we could not complete our journey there, we are continuing in this solar system.

Our Objective

As we saw in the previous chapter, our objective, in the human kingdom is to reach the fifth initiation and achieve *moksha* or liberation – this is when the higher soul becomes perfect and merges with the divine spark.

There is a time frame for this. We need to achieve this objective by the end of this chain. The good news is that since we are just halfway through this chain, we have literally millions and millions of years to achieve the objective. However, we cannot be complacent because evolution takes time, it can take thousands of lifetimes to achieve *moksha*.

A first initiate is called *sotapanna* or 'he who enters the stream.' The stream referred to is the stream of spiritual life, which is definitely entered at the first initiation. Once we have entered this stream, i.e., once we achieve the first initiation, it is more or less certain that we will be able to continue with our evolution and achieve liberation well before the end of our chain-period.

Judgement Day

The concept of Judgement Day is linked to the timeline discussed above. Imagine that the chain period is like one year in school. Our objective, becoming a fifth initiate, is like graduating from our current grade, to move to the next grade.

Imagine a student who is lagging behind his classmates, somewhere in the school year, the teachers realise that he is not going to be able to pass, despite their best efforts and the student's best efforts.

Instead of struggling through the rest of the year, being unable to complete assignments and failing the exam, the teachers decide to give the student some time off, so he can join the same grade again the next year. Though this may delay his graduation, it is easier and less stressful for the student; it also enables his classmates to move further and faster, since the teachers do not have to slow down to help the lagging student.

In the same way, if some human souls are seen to be lagging behind the majority of humanity, and the Spiritual Teachers of the human race realise that this soul is not going to achieve the fifth initiation in this chain, they take that soul out of the evolutionary process in our chain. The soul will continue its evolution elsewhere.

This decision is not taken lightly, and it will not be taken now. According to the teachings, this decision will be taken around the middle of the fifth round of our chain (millions of years in the future). At that time, if the Spiritual Teachers feel that some souls will not be able to achieve the objective, they will move those souls out of our evolutionary scheme (and into another evolutionary scheme).

This is what is commonly known as Judgement Day. However, Judgement Day is not a day when some will be eternally damned. Far from it, Theosophy assures us that each and every soul will eventually achieve the objective of liberation. No one will be left behind, not one single soul. The only question is when we will achieve the objective of liberation.

Will we achieve it by the end of this chain, as per the objective given to us? Will we have to wait for a future time, or will we be able to achieve the objective much earlier? That is in our hands. Our evolution, our spiritual progress, is in our hands and no one else's. Each one of us, and no one else, has control over our progress.

God has created an entire evolutionary scheme to help us achieve our objective of liberation. We are assured that each and every one of us **will** achieve liberation. When we achieve it, is in our hands.

Chapter 9
Conclusion

Since the founding of the Theosophical Society in 1875 by H P Blavatsky and H S Olcott, many people and many other schools have been guided and inspired by these teachings. Great teachers like Alice Bailey and Rudolf Steiner, to name a couple, have been part of, or inspired by the Theosophical teachings.

Understanding the concepts and terms explained in this book will help the reader understand many other books, books by the Theosophical Society and books by other schools (such as Astara, Lucis Trust, Torkom Saraydarian and others) more easily.

Theosophy answers many questions that we have, such as, "Why are we here? What is the objective of life? Where did we come from? Where do we go after we die? Is there a purpose to life? How do we achieve our objective as a soul?"

Not only do we find many answers in the teachings of Theosophy, but the teachings are also incredibly uplifting. We are assured that each and every one of us, human, animal, plant and mineral, all consciousness, will eventually achieve the goal – whatever the goal is at that level of consciousness.

No one fails, no one is eternally damned, there is no eternal hell. We will all eventually succeed. The only question is, when. And that, dear readers, is entirely in our hands.

I hope this book helps you to get started (or inspires you to continue) on the path of *jnana yoga* – spiritual development through study and knowledge. I hope it inspires you to go on and read the many incredible books written by the teachers of the Theosophical Society and gain from their tremendous knowledge and wisdom.

However, let us not forget that the teachings, while an important part of our spiritual journey, are not the only factor. The Teacher and our spiritual community are equally important.

As the Three Jewels of Buddhism state:
I take refuge in the Teacher,
I take refuge in the Teachings,
I take refuge in the spiritual community.

May these Three Jewels guide, nurture and inspire us all, throughout our spiritual journey, leading to the ultimate objective – *moksha*.

The Divinity in me, recognises and salutes the Divinity within you.
Atma namaste!

Bibliography

C. W. Leadbeater, *A Textbook of Theosophy* (Theosophical Publishing Society, 1912)

Annie Besant, *A Study in Consciousness*, (Theosophical Publishing Society, 1915)

Recommended Reading

Achieving Oneness with the Higher Soul	Grand Master Choa Kok Sui
A Textbook of Theosophy	C W Leadbeater
A Study in Consciousness	Annie Besant
The Etheric Double	Arthur Powell
The Astral Body	Arthur Powell
The Mental Body	Arthur Powell
The Causal Body	Arthur Powell
Masters and the Path	C W Leadbeater
The Science of Yoga	I K Taimni
Yogic Ascent to Spiritual Heights	Geoffrey Hodson
The Existence of God is Self-Evident	Grand Master Choa Kok Sui

Grand Master Choa Kok Sui

Grand Master Choa Kok Sui is the founder of Modern Pranic Healing and Arhatic Yoga. A chemical engineer by education and a businessman by profession, Grand Master Choa Kok Sui (or GMCKS as he is known to his students) is also a spiritual teacher to thousands, a master healer, a philanthropist, and a best-selling author. Truly a modern-day renaissance man.

He established the Institute for Inner Studies Inc. in 1987, in Manila, Philippines followed by the World Pranic Healing Foundation Inc. in 1990 to spread his teachings worldwide.

When he was asked (during the First World Pranic Healers Convention in Manila in 1996), why he established the school, his answer was that he saw people around the world struggling with problems in four main areas – health, relationships, finances and facing a sense of spiritual emptiness. His objective was to provide solutions to these problems that we face – Pranic Healing for health, techniques to help and heal relationships, Kriyashakti for prosperity and Arhatic Yoga for spiritual development.

One of the amazing aspects of GMCKS' teachings is the breadth and depth of information that that they contain, explained in simple language. One of his skills has been to take complex topics and explain them in a very simple way.

The organisations he established, including many charitable organisations around the world, continue to grow, spreading his teachings and reaching out to people all over the world.

Author Bio

Sriram Rajagopal started his journey in Pranic Healing in February 1993, while he was still a university student. Upon completion of his studies in Physics and Computer Science, he was appointed as a Trustee and the General Manager of World Pranic Healing Foundation India by Grand Master Choa Kok Sui.

He worked closely with GMCKS for several years, accompanying him on all his trips in India as well as a few trips in other countries, receiving personal guidance and training in many areas.

Always an avid reader, Sriram started reading books on spirituality in his teens. After learning Pranic Healing, he used to visit the bookstore in the headquarters of the Theosophical Society in Adyar, Chennai to buy many of their publications. He has read multiple books on Theosophy, many of them several times as well as books on related topics by Torkom Saraydarian, Alice Bailey, Astara and many others.

He brings his knowledge of Theosophy and a scientific background to explain complex ideas in a clear manner, using simple language, following the style of his Teacher, Grand Master Choa Kok Sui.

Currently, Sriram teaches extensively across India, the Middle East, and Africa, parts of South Asia and Southeast Asia and he continues to work for the World Pranic Healing Foundation.

27301484R10075